Contents

Acknowledgement

All Praise and thanks be to Allah! We praise and thank Him, ask Him for His Help and Forgiveness, and we seek refuge in Allah from the evils of our souls and the mischiefs of our deeds. He whom Allah guides will not be misled, and he whom Allah misleads will never have a guide. I testify that there is no deity but Allah alone, without any partners, and that Muhammad is His 'Abd (worshiper) and Messenger.

Putting together a work of this nature is a monumental task that obviously takes more effort than that of a translator and editor. As is always, to mention all those who aided us with their various input would be an equally lengthy task. But, of course, a few people stand out for their significant commitment in making this book a success.

We would first like to thank Br. Muhammed Al-Jibaly for reading the Arabic text and pointing out subtle changes in the English translation. Also, we thank Saffet Abid Catovic and Basit Koshul for reading the manuscript and advising us on how to make it more readable and understandable. A special thanks goes out to Muhammed Hozien for his general help and for translating and organizing the page titles. We also thank Shouaib Designers for donating the cover design. Of course, first and last, all praise and thanks are due to Allah (swt), may He (awj) forgive us for any mistakes and show us the right path.

Abdallah M. Mekkaoui
Jameel D. Pavlin
June 16, 1987

Preface

Al-'Uboodiyah , literally, is that state in which a person subdues himself with humility and love to the will of someone else. One can easily enslave himself to any created being. This type of *'Uboodiyah* surely leads to sadness, humiliation, and transgression; it is then the enslavement by false idols. But devoting oneself to the Creator (swt) of all the beings and submitting to His (awj) Command leads to nothing but happiness, nobility and justice; and that is the beloved *'Uboodiyah*.

The reader may know that the word 'Abd in Arabic carries the meaning of both "slave" and "worshiper." In this treatise, Ibn Taymiyah clarified successfully not only the distinction between being a "slave" and being a "worshiper," but also enlightened us to the full scope of what worship in Islam is.

We are all aware of the horrors and atrocities of human enslavement perpetrated throughout the history of the human race. In the case of divine enslavement, *Al-'Uboodiyah* represents the human beings' "slavery" to Allah (awj), our devotion and submission to our Lord and Creator. It, therefore, becomes necessary to make sure we are aware of the distinctions between human enslavement and divine enslavement. The latter type of *'Uboodiyah* is a slavery which is beloved. It frees us from idolatry and saves us from the evils of "Taaghoot" (he who sets himself up as an object of worship). In this case, *Al 'Uboodiyah* corresponds to happiness and virtue and brings back to man his nobility and excellence.

Being in this *'Uboodiyah*, we prostrate before Allah (swt), we do not become humiliated before any tyrant on earth, and we walk on the path of goodness until victory or martyrdom. If people were to respond to this noble *Da'wah* (call), they would live in freedom, virtue, happiness and peace. But Ibn Taymiyah did not stop at this general understanding of *'Uboodiyah*. He went on to clarify the subtle yet powerful distinctions between mere "slavery" and true "worship." To accomplish this he articulated his ideas by extracting evidence from the legislated texts (Quran and Sunnah). Also, he highlighted his presentation of the truth by using linguistic arguments as to how to understand the texts, and supported his propositions with uncontested scientific, psychological and sociological facts which are still valid today. All this led to a most in-depth and comprehensive study of worship in Islam.

The main point of his theology is that all created things (organic and inorganic) are 'Ibaad-Allah (slaves of Allah), but that the 'Ibaad are immediately divided into two groups: one being the involuntary slaves and the other being the voluntary slaves. Obviously, animals, plants and minerals fall under the first category while the human beings are free to choose their position.

In other words, there are two different realities - the Universal Reality and the Religious Reality. All Ibaad (slaves) are subject to the Universal Reality. Whether one is good or bad, believer or disbeliever, or rich or poor, he is subject to the laws of physics (i.e. the sun shines on us all). The Religious Reality, however, is the voluntary acceptance of Allah's legislation and willingly struggling to love and obey Allah (swt), His Messenger (saw) and the Message of Al Islam. It is the true 'Abd (worshiper) who recognizes the two Realities, keeps them clear in his mind, and strives to fulfill the dictates of the Religious Reality - Allah's (swt) Commands. This, then, explains why, in a religious context, 'Abd is sometimes translated as slave, and other times as worshiper. It is the choice to follow Islam that makes the 'Abd (slave) become an 'Abd (worshiper).

After establishing this point, Ibn Taymiyah then went on to explain how various groups of Muslims misunderstood this, misinterpreted it, or simply twisted it for their own benefit. It is the complete or partial confusion of the Universal Reality with the Religious Reality that has given birth to deviation from the straight path and weakness in the moral fibre of mankind. The theology propounded by Ibn Taymiyah, the theology of Quran and Sunnah, is the means of reforming the soul and rejuvenating the Spirit of man to walk in the light of Al-Islaam. Ibn Taymiyah has explained away the many forms of misguidance into which man fell, and has given us a theology to reform our intellectual and disciplinary behaviour. He has warned us of theories that propagate so-called elite statuses for their followers, theories that would actually lead us astray. He has thus slammed shut the doors through which came the evils of astray desires, phoney philosophies, anarchic methodologies and deviated meanings of Allah's (swt) Words and Commands. To help us understand Ibn Taymiyah's treatise there are several thoughts to keep in mind.

Ibn Taymiyah unveiled for us a whole process whereby the first small step towards deviation, whether intentional or not, leads further and further down the path of Shirk (associating partners with Allah swt,) and *Kufr* (denying the truth). He first warned us against falling prey to the teachings of those who claim to have witnessed the truth. Basically, this is where one would experience a phenomenon in the realm of the Universal Reality and take it as a sign that he is on a select path of truth. He witnesses the Universal Reality, stops there and does not establish that duty to fulfill the Religious Reality. He believes in Allah (swt), but only admitting that all things are willed by Allah, and that all events and phenomena fall under Al-Qadar (the Divine Measure). This allows for the emergence of the doctrine of fatalism and the suspension of the duties legislated by Allah (swt). Here, the person embarking on this path thinks that if he commits a sin it is simply because Allah has willed it for him. Fatalism leads to a silence towards evil and excuses for shirk. The human being becomes a helpless puppet.

The next step becomes the admission of *Wahdat Al Wuujuud* (unifying of existence). The absurd logic of the deviant mind rationalizes that since Allah is the one absolute, and all things occur by the will of Allah, then all things must be an extension of Allah. By taking that first step in denying the Religious Realities, the astray man now has committed a worse form of *Kufr* than Ahl Al-Kitaab (people of the Scripture) and the Mushrikeen (idolators). He has, in effect, set himself up as part of the Godhead and has made allowable all actions whether sinful or otherwise. By using the undeniable proofs of Quran and Sunnah, Ibn Taymiyah unveiled how these astray sects adopted an inverted meaning of *Al 'Uboodiyah* and showed their lack of true understanding of Al-Islam.

Finally, Ibn Taymiyah explained the defects in the thinking of the two major sects that evolved out of this false interpretation of Al-Qadar. The explanation of the deviant sect just given describes the beliefs of Al Jabriyah. This group affirms the existence of Al Qadha, the Divine Decree and Al-Qadar, the Divine Measure. When we say the "Measure" we mean the good and evil that Allah (swt) has measured out for us. But in the face of this, Al-Jabriyah denied the legislated commanding of good and forbidding of evil. This occurred because they were too narrow-minded to understand how Allah (swt) could command one thing (good) but measure out something else (e.g. evil).

They therefore rationalized that there is only the Divine Measure, and the Commands and Prohibitions do not apply. But as is made clear by Ibn Taymiyah, all things are indeed willed by Allah (awj), but, equally important, Allah (awj) loves for us to - in fact prefers that we - follow that which is right and good and avoid that which is evil and wrong. For this very reason the Quran was sent down to us.

What does Allah (swt) say in Surat Al-Fatihah? Is it not "Show us the straight path, the path of those whom You have blessed, not of those who receive Your Wrath, or of those who went astray." Also, in the opening of Surat Al-Baqarah does it not state - "This is the Book, without doubt there is in it guidance for those who ward off evil."

The question is, what do you do when you show someone a path or give someone guidance? Are they then forced, with no choice whatsoever, to do your bidding? Certainly not! So, also, Allah (swt) does not lead us to good or evil without it being based on His Perfect Wisdom and Justice. The choice is ours, and He (awj) guides us to that which is right.

So, Al-Jabriyah went off into Al-Qadar and lost sight of the Divine Legislation. In response to them there developed other groups such as Al-Qadariyah and Al Mu'tazilah. The latter group, Al-Mu'tazilah, typifies the thinking of Al-Qadariyah in general. In effect they reversed the rationalization of Al-Jabriyah. They affirmed the Commands and Prohibitions but denied the Divine Decree and Measure. Whereas Al- Jabriyah stripped Allah (awj) of His Right of Legislation, Al Mu'tazilah stripped Him (swt) of His Most Perfect Will. Both groups have erred to the point of committing *Kufr*. (This does not mean we can declare them Kafir, but we must be aware of their astray beliefs.)

As Ibn Taymiyah points out, this is nothing but pure lies that conceal their *Kufr* beliefs.

Ibn Taymiyah then went on to prove that to realize *Al 'Uboodiyah* one must go the way of *Ash- Sharee'ah* (Divine Legislation). To worship Allah (awj) correctly we must worship Him according to His path, and that is to follow the Legislated Path - Ash Sharee'ah. Ibn Taymiyah took the *Shahaadatain* (Testimonies of Faith) and linked them to two basic principles of Islam. As we know, "*La ilaaha illa Allah*" implies that none are to be worshipped except Allah (swt). And "Muhammad Rasool-Allah" implies that the theme of the Message is to clarify the way in which we worship and that any deviation is inherently in opposition to Ash-Sharee'ah.

To this is linked two conditions that must be fulfilled to establish true worship. First, we must perform righteous deeds knowing that a deed cannot be righteous unless it complies with the Legislation of Allah (swt) as sent down to His Rasool (saw). Second, when performing the deed nothing is to be sought from it except the pleasure of Allah (awj). In this way Ibn Taymiyah instructed us, as is stated in Quran, that selectivity in the Deen of Islam is wrong. We cannot pick out parts and reject other parts, but we must accept the whole of Islam as it is. This becomes the essence of perfecting our worship.

A Word On Style

Whenever one attempts to translate a text various problems naturally occur. Languages are very distinctive and each has its own set of idioms, phrases and expressions. Thus a translator must often reject a literal translation for the sake of presenting the proper meaning. When you add to this the fact that Ibn Taymiyah was a great scholar of the highest caliber and that he wrote over 600 years ago, the translation process becomes even trickier. In this translation we decided to stick as close to the original text as possible. We did this for various reasons. First of all, we felt it is important to introduce the reader to Ibn Taymiyah's thinking process. Not only was his form and style logical and concise, but his very use of certain words and expressions carried significant meaning and importance. Why a particular word is used when others may be equally interchangeable says something of the author's concepts and beliefs. This does create, however, a small problem for someone living in twentieth-century America. So we warn you that some sentences and paragraphs may come across as being awkward and archaic. We ask you to read carefully and reflect on the content of the text.

As for Ibn Taymiyah's style, you will notice that much of the book is quoted from Al-Quran. He (RA) presented his argument and point of view and then supported it with a list of evidences. Also, he drifts slightly from his main theme when a sub-topic becomes vital as clarification of the main point. Do not be surprised if you find yourself somewhat lost as to the point he was trying to make. As you read on he brings you back to his original point but now with a deeper understanding. Again, you may have to read over certain passages several times before grasping the meaning. May Allah (swt) accept this work from us and make it a means of spreading Deen Al-Islam. May He (awj) grant you patience and understanding and allow you to benefit from this book. May Allah (swt} bless us all and guide us on His (awj) Straight Path.

Ibn Taymiyah

The truth had been mixed with falsehood, the insight had been confused with ignorance, and As-Sunnah had been defeated by Al-Bid'ah. The Muslims were wandering in the matters of their beliefs. Their strength had been enfeebled by the fighting amongst those with astray scholastic opinions, and their personalities had been weakened by straying away from their Deen.

The Muslims found their way into illusions and heresies and considered all of that as part of Ad-Deen. They were an easy prey for the external transgressing invaders, At-Tataar, and the internal oppressing tyrants and their scholastic agents.

It was the seventh century of Al-Hijrah. The era was awaiting a true scholar to reform the social, economical, intellectual, moral, and political life. A true scholar was needed to illuminate for the: Muslims the way out of the darkness of Sufism and scholasticism and to shine the glow of Al-Qur'aan and As-Sunnah on their path. The Muslims were in need of a true scholar who would not only live amongst his books, who would not be only satisfied with his compilations, and who would not look at the people from his ivory tower. But, they were in need of a scholar who would advance to the front carrying the flag of Al-Jihaad and would care little about what he received of torture, imprisonment, or death. The Muslims were in need of a true scholar to dis-illusion them from Al-Bid'ah and reconstruct their personalities in the light of Al-Quran and As-Sunnah to defend their Deen and their Ummah. They were in need of Ibn Taymiyah!

Childhood and Early Years

The family of Ibn Taymiyah had at that time, in the country of Ash-Shaam, a very wide reputation in knowledge and leadership in the different Islamic sciences. Sheikh Al-Islam Majd Ad-Deen Abd As Salaam, the grandfather of Ibn Taymiyah, was unique in his era, a leader in jurisprudence and its principles, very talented in the Hadeeth and its sciences, and very knowledgeable in the different recitations of Al Quran and its exegesis. Sheikh Shihaab Ad-Deen Abd Al-Haleem, Ibn Taymiyah's father, was a prominent Imaam in the jurisprudence according to the discipline of Imaam Ahmad bin Hanbal. He was also a renowned scholar in many other Islamic sciences. He became the Sheikh of a Hadeeth school in Damascus after he migrated there from Harraan with his family during the tribulation of At-Tataar. He also held a chair in the great Masjid of Damascus during Fridays.

Taqee Ad-Deen Ahmad bin Abd Al-Haleem bin Abd As-Salaam bin Taymiyah, the grandson and the famous scholar was born in Harraan in the year 661 A.H./1263 C.E. He lived there until the age of seven when he fled to Damascus with his family to escape from the horrid aggression of At-Tataar. In Damascus he took up the memorization of the Quran and an in depth study of Al-Hadeeth. As a young man he was noted for his unusual alertness of mind, quickness of perception, and an acutely sharp memory. To become an Aalim was a natural pursuit for him because he came from a family of many renowned scholars. He astonished his teachers and masters with his great memorization capability and his brightness.

In his early teens he mastered the fundamentals of Ad Deen and gained a great share of knowledge of At Tafseer, Al-Hadeeth, and the Arabic language. In his youth he used to attend the circles of the 'Ulamaa, debate with them, and convince the best of them to his position. He started giving Fataawa (juridical opinions) when he was nineteen. He lectured, relying on his memory, on Tafseer on Fridays as his father used to do.

He inclined towards Al-Hadeeth and its sciences. He heard from more than two hundred of its scholars, and attained a vast knowledge of these sciences. His memory was so great that he would not forget anything even if he passed over it quickly. He also had a great talent and ability of referring to the Quranic verses and using them to prove his arguments.

Political and Social Conditions of His Era.

Ibn Al-Atheer described the political and military conditions prevailing in the Muslim world during Ibn Taymiyah's lifetime in the following words:

"Islam and Muslims had during that period been afflicted by such disasters that no other nation had experienced. One such affliction was the invasion by At-Tataar. They came from the east and inflicted overwhelming damages. Another was the onset of the Frankish people (the Crusaders) from the West to Mesopotamia and Egypt, they occupied its ports, and nearly subjected all of Egypt to their rule, had it not been for Allah's Mercy and victory over them. But another affliction was that the Muslims themselves had been divided, and their swords lifted up against their fellows.

"In addition to such horrid conditions facing the Muslims on the political and military front, Islam as practiced and preached by Prophet Muhammad (saw) and As-Salaf As-Saalih (the righteous predecessors) was being seriously challenged by various deviant sects. The Sufi movement which was spear-headed by the teachings of Al-Ghazali had won over many converts and was exercising a firm hold on the intellect and patterns of thought of many people. Along with this Al-Ash'ari system of creed had been widely accepted by the majority of the scholars of Ibn Taymiyah's day. Al-Ash'ari system of doctrine was a mixture of the Salafi methodology which is based on revelation centered theology and the Mu'tazilah methodology which is based on a rationalist thought system.

"Taqleed was practiced widely. Even though information on the Deen, Fiqh, Ahaadeeth, etc., was abundantly available, only a handful of scholars and ordinary people took up the task of investigating the sources of the knowledge and its vehicle. Most people blindly accepted the teaching of their Sheikh or Imaam without questioning or investigating the sources from where the knowledge had come."

His Contributions

This was the dreary condition of the Muslim world during Ibn Taymiyah's era, and it was this condition that he sought to improve. He was very active in defending the Deen both intellectually and actively. Almost all of his works are a critique or refutation of un-Islamic ideas which had crept into the Deen or a defense of certain points which he felt needed to be brought to the attention of the Muslim Ummah.

The active role he played in defending the Deen is best exemplified by Ibn Taymiyah's activity during At Tataar invasion of the Muslim lands. During this crucial period in Islamic history he provided indispensable ideological and military inspiration. He expounded on the virtues of Al-Jihaad, declaring it to be the most urgent duty. Using his gifts of the tongue and pen he bolstered the morale of the Muslims and took this opportunity to bring into focus their conception of unity, their understanding of Islam and Eemaan, and their view of Allah (swt) as well as their religious and social self-awareness.

On the military field Ibn Taymiyah persuaded the Egyptians to send support troops to Syria which was then under attack by At-Tataar - telling them that it was their Islamic duty to do so. Afterwards he joined the battle against At-Tataar and Allah (swt) granted the Muslims the victory. During the battle Ibn Taymiyah was always to be seen in the front lines fighting the Kuffaar and his valor and bravery during the battle of Shaqhab, 702 A.H./1304 C.E., became legendary.

He defended Ad-Deen not only on the military front but also on the ideological one. Ibn Taymiyah's major enemies on the ideological front were the Sufis and the scholasticists.

He abhorred the Sufi ideas of pantheism, agnosticism, and a deterministic view of total religious resignation. According to him the implication of these ideas upon the Muslim community were devastating because they led to political apathy, religious misconceptions, and withdrawal from an active community life. A major portion of his intellectual energies was spent refuting the doctrine of the Sufis.

The Shee'ah were also subjected to harsh criticism by Ibn Taymiyah because of the many flaws in their doctrines and beliefs. He strongly denounced their falsification of the historical facts and forging of the Sunnah to support their own political views.

Ibn Taymiyah also attacked Al-Jahamiyah and Al Jabriyah - the determinists - who denied the human being's responsibility for any of his actions. He also denounced Al-Mu'tazilah and Al-Qadariyah - the rationalists - who held human free will as the basis of human action. He also did doctrinal battle with the followers of Abu Al-Hasan Al- Ash'ari- on various issues including determinism/free will, the Attributes of Allah (awj), and other issues of the Islamic creed.

As a result of his confrontation with the Sufis and the scholasticists, he made many enemies among them. Many of their leaders who exercised political clout used it against him and as a result he was once exiled in Alexandria and imprisoned on three different occasions. His writings were banned and during the last of his three imprisonments he was forbidden to read, write or communicate with family and friends.

Ibn Taymiyah gave himself relentlessly to pointing the way to the knowledge which, in his own words, means: "The Prophet has shown the fundamentals and applications of religion, its intent as well as its expression, its (intellectual) knowledge and its action. This fact is the foundation of all fundamental knowledge and belief; and he who most adheres to this foundation is most worthy of the truth - both to know it and to do it."

His Death

Ibn Taymiyah felt that imprisonment for knowledge constituted alternate freedom, and he welcomed imprisonment as an opportunity to think and to work. But when his books were taken away and he was not allowed to commit to writing his beliefs - as was the case during his last imprisonment - this was the severest punishment for him. As a result he passed away in his cell in Damascus, in 728 A.H./ 1328 C.E.

Commenting on the attacks on him by his enemies, Ibn Taymiyah commented: "In this life is a paradise which must be entered before that of the life to come can be enjoyed: What could my enemies have done to me? My heaven and paradise is in my breast; wherever I go it accompanies me. My imprisonment is only an opportunity to be alone; my murder is only a testimony; my exile from my country is a holiday." During his last imprisonment Taqee Ad-Deen Ibn Taymiyah made this Du'aa to Allah (swt): "Almighty Allah, assist me to remember Thy goodness, to thank Thee and genuinely to worship Thee, according to Thy will."

Definition of worship, its branches, and it's aspects

In the Name of Allah, Most Gracious, Most Merciful. Praise and thanks be to Allah! We praise and thank Him, ask Him for His Help and Forgiveness, and we seek refuge in Allah from the evils of our souls and the mischiefs of our deeds. He whom Allah guides will not be misled, and he whom Allah misleads will never have a guide. I testify that there is no deity but Allah alone, without any partners, and that Muhammad is His 'Abd (worshiper) and Messenger.(1) To proceed,

Sheikh Al-Islam, the famous amongst the famous, protector of As-Sunnah, suppressor of Al-Bid'ah (innovation in Ad-Deen), Ahmad bin Abd Al-Haleem bin Taymiyah (RA) was asked the following about Allah's (awj) saying,

يَا أَيُّهَا النَّاسُ اعْبُدُوا رَبَّكُمُ

"Oh mankind! worship your Lord."   [Al-Baqarah:21]

What is Al-'Ibaadah (the worship)? What are its branches? Is the whole of Ad-Deen encompassed in it? What is the reality of *Al-'Uboodiyah* ? And is it the highest attainable position in this world and in the Hereafter or if there is any rank better than it? Please expound upon that.

Ibn Taymiyah (RA) replied,

Al-'Ibaadah is a term which comprises everything that Allah (swt) loves and approves of from the apparent and hidden sayings and deeds. In this context As-Salaat (prayer); Az-Zakaat (charity tax); As-Siyaam (fasting); Al-Hajj (pilgrimage); truthfulness in speech; trustworthiness; kindness to parents; maintaining kind relationship with relatives; fulfilling pledges; enjoining the good and forbidding the evil; striving against Al-Kuffaar (the faith rejectors) and the hypocrites; beneficence to the neighbor, the orphan, the poor, the wayfarer, and the owned beings whether human or animal; Ad-Du'aa (supplication); Adth-Dthikr (remembrance of Allah); Al-Qiraa-ah (recitation of Al-Quran); and the like are all part of Al-'Ibaadah.

Likewise, loving Allah (awj) and His Messenger (saw), apprehension before Allah and returning repentantly to Him, sincerity in Ad-Deen for Him, patience with His Ordainment, thankfulness for His Bounties, contentment with His Decree, dependence on Him, hope for His Mercy, fear of His Punishment and the like are also part of Al-'Ibaadah due to Allah (swt).

In fact worshipping Allah (awj) is the beloved purpose before Him, and which contents Him, it being the reason for which He (swt) created the creation. As Allah (awj) said,

وَمَا خَلَقْتُ الْجِنَّ وَالْإِنسَ إِلَّا لِيَعْبُدُونِ

"And I created not the Jinns and men except that they should worship Me (Alone)."   [Adth- Dthaariyaat:56]

This paragraph is not in all the manuscripts. It is a portion from the Speech of Need which Rasool- Allah (saw) used to open his speeches with and Sheikh Al-Islam Ibn Taymiyah often used to open hs speeches with in compliance with As Sunnah. See "KhutbatAI-Haajah" by AI-Muhaddith As-Sheikh Muhammad Naasir Ad-Deen Al-Albaani.

The call of the Prophets to worship Allah (awj)

With this call to Al-'Ibaadah He (swt) sent all the Messengers as when Prophet Nooh (AS) said to his people,

اعْبُدُوا اللَّهَ مَا لَكُم مِّنْ إِلَهٍ غَيْرُهُ

"Worship Allah, you have no other deity but Him." [Al-A'raaf:59]

And similarly Hood, Saalih, Shou'eyb (AS) and other Prophets said this to their people. Allah (swt) (the Exalted) said,

وَلَقَدْ بَعَثْنَا فِي كُلِّ أُمَّةٍ رَّسُولًا أَنِ اعْبُدُوا اللَّهَ وَاجْتَنِبُوا الطَّاغُوتَ ۖ فَمِنْهُم مَّنْ هَدَى اللَّهُ وَمِنْهُم مَّنْ حَقَّتْ عَلَيْهِ الضَّلَالَةُ ۚ فَسِيرُوا فِي الْأَرْضِ فَانظُرُوا كَيْفَ كَانَ عَاقِبَةُ الْمُكَذِّبِينَ

" And We certainly sent into every nation a messenger, [saying], "Worship Allah and avoid Taghut." And among them were those whom Allah guided, and among them were those upon whom error was [deservedly] decreed. "

[An-Nahl: 36]

None has the right to be worshipped but Allah (swt)

He (swt) also said.

وَمَا أَرْسَلْنَا مِن قَبْلِكَ مِن رَّسُولٍ إِلَّا نُوحِي إِلَيْهِ أَنَّهُ لَا إِلَهَ إِلَّا أَنَا فَاعْبُدُونِ

"And We did not send any messenger before you (O Muhammad) but We revealed unto him (saying): 'There is none who has the right to be worshipped but I (Allah), so worship Me (Alone and none else).'" [Al-Anbiyaa:25];

and

إِنَّ هَذِهِ أُمَّتُكُمْ أُمَّةً وَاحِدَةً وَأَنَا رَبُّكُمْ فَاعْبُدُونِ

"Truly, your Nation (Deen of Islam) is one Nation and I am your Lord, therefore worship Me (Alone)." [Al-Anbiyaa:92];

also He (swt) said in another Aayah (verse),

يَا أَيُّهَا الرُّسُلُ كُلُوا مِنَ الطَّيِّبَاتِ وَاعْمَلُوا صَالِحًا ۖ إِنِّي بِمَا تَعْمَلُونَ عَلِيمٌ -
وَإِنَّ هَذِهِ أُمَّتُكُمْ أُمَّةً وَاحِدَةً وَأَنَا رَبُّكُمْ فَاتَّقُونِ

"O (you) Messengers! Eat of the good things and do righteous deeds; verily I am well-acquainted with all that you do. And verily! This your Nation is one Nation and I am your Lord, therefore seek protection (from My Punishment by warding off evil)." [Al Moominoon: 51-52]

Describing 'Ibaad-u-Ar-Rahmaan with *Al-'Uboodiyah*

Allah (swt) has made Al-'Ibaadah imperative on His Messenger until death. He (awj) said.

$$\text{وَاعْبُدْ رَبَّكَ حَتَّىٰ يَأْتِيَكَ الْيَقِينُ}$$

"And worship your Lord (O Muhammad) until there comes unto you the Hour that is certain (i.e. death)."　　　　[Al-Hijr:99]

By this qualifying distinction (Al-'Ibaadah) Allah (awj) described His Angels and Prophets. He (awj) said,

$$\text{وَلَهُ مَن فِي السَّمَاوَاتِ وَالْأَرْضِ ۚ وَمَنْ عِندَهُ لَا يَسْتَكْبِرُونَ عَنْ عِبَادَتِهِ وَلَا}$$

$$\text{يَسْتَحْسِرُونَ - يُسَبِّحُونَ اللَّيْلَ وَالنَّهَارَ لَا يَفْتُرُونَ}$$

"To Him belongs whosoever is in the heavens and the earth. And those who are in His very presence (the Angels) disdain not to worship Him, nor do they ever weary in this. They exalt Him night and day (and) they never slacken (to do so)." [Al-Anbiyaa: 19 - 20];

and,

$$\text{إِنَّ الَّذِينَ عِندَ رَبِّكَ لَا يَسْتَكْبِرُونَ عَنْ عِبَادَتِهِ وَيُسَبِّحُونَهُ وَلَهُ يَسْجُدُونَ}$$

"Surely those who are in the very presence of your Lord disdain not

to worship Him; they celebrate His praises, and prostrate before Him." [Al-A'raaf:206]

Allah (swt) disgraced those who are disdainful of Al-'Ibaadah by saying,

وَقَالَ رَبُّكُمُ ادْعُونِي أَسْتَجِبْ لَكُمْ ۚ إِنَّ الَّذِينَ يَسْتَكْبِرُونَ عَنْ عِبَادَتِي سَيَدْخُلُونَ جَهَنَّمَ دَاخِرِينَ

"And your Lord said: 'Invoke Me, and I will respond to your (invocation). Verily! those who scorn My worship, they will surely enter Hell in humiliation!'"

[Al-Moo-min:60]

Describing the best of His (awj) creatures

Allah (swt) also described the best of His creatures with *Al-
'Uboodiyah* to Him by saying.

إِنَّ الْأَبْرَارَ يَشْرَبُونَ مِن كَأْسٍ كَانَ مِزَاجُهَا كَافُورًا – عَيْنًا يَشْرَبُ بِهَا عِبَادُ اللَّهِ يُفَجِّرُونَهَا تَفْجِيرًا

*"As to the righteous, they shall drink of a cup containing a mixture
of Kaafoor. A fountain where 'Ibaad- u-Allah (worshipers of Allah)
do drink, making it flow in unstinted abundance."* [Ad-Dahr:5-
6]

and

وَعِبَادُ الرَّحْمَٰنِ الَّذِينَ يَمْشُونَ عَلَى الْأَرْضِ هَوْنًا وَإِذَا خَاطَبَهُمُ الْجَاهِلُونَ قَالُوا سَلَامًا

*"And 'Ibaad-u-Ar-Rahmaan (the worshipers of the Most Beneficent;
Allah) are those who walk on the earth in humility, and when the
foolish address them, they say 'Peace (on you)!"* [Al-Furqaan:63]

And when Ash-Shaitaan (Satan) said.

قَالَ رَبِّ بِمَا أَغْوَيْتَنِي لَأُزَيِّنَنَّ لَهُمْ فِي الْأَرْضِ وَلَأُغْوِيَنَّهُمْ أَجْمَعِينَ – إِلَّا عِبَادَكَ

مِنْهُمُ الْمُخْلَصِينَ

"O my Lord! Because You misled me I shall indeed adorn the path of error for them (mankind) on earth and I shall mislead them all. Except Your chosen, guided 'Ibaad among them." [Al-Hijr: 39-40]

Then Allah (swt) replied

إِنَّ عِبَادِي لَيْسَ لَكَ عَلَيْهِمْ سُلْطَانٌ إِلَّا مَنِ اتَّبَعَكَ مِنَ الْغَاوِينَ

"Certainly, you have no authority over 'Ibaad-ee (My worshipers), except those who follow you of the wrong-doers." [AI-Hijr:42]

Describing the Angels with *Al-'Uboodiyah*

Also, in describing the Angels with *Al-'Uboodiyah* He (awj) said,

وَقَالُوا اتَّخَذَ الرَّحْمَٰنُ وَلَدًا ۗ سُبْحَانَهُ ۚ بَلْ عِبَادٌ مُّكْرَمُونَ – لَا يَسْبِقُونَهُ بِالْقَوْلِ وَهُم بِأَمْرِهِ يَعْمَلُونَ – يَعْلَمُ مَا بَيْنَ أَيْدِيهِمْ وَمَا خَلْفَهُمْ وَلَا يَشْفَعُونَ إِلَّا لِمَنِ ارْتَضَىٰ وَهُم مِّنْ خَشْيَتِهِ مُشْفِقُونَ

*"And they say; The Beneficient (Allah) has begotten children.'
Exalted be He! Those whom they call children, (i.e. the Angels), are
but honored 'Ibaad. They speak not until He has spoken, and they
act by His Command. He knows what is before them, and what is
behind them, and they cannot intercede except for him with whom
He is pleased. And they stand in awe due to their apprehension of
Him."* [Al Anbiya:26 - 28]

He (swt) also said,

وَقَالُوا اتَّخَذَ الرَّحْمَٰنُ وَلَدًا – لَّقَدْ جِئْتُمْ شَيْئًا إِدًّا – تَكَادُ السَّمَاوَاتُ يَتَفَطَّرْنَ مِنْهُ وَتَنشَقُّ الْأَرْضُ وَتَخِرُّ الْجِبَالُ هَدًّا – أَن دَعَوْا لِلرَّحْمَٰنِ وَلَدًا – وَمَا يَنبَغِي لِلرَّحْمَٰنِ أَن يَتَّخِذَ وَلَدًا – إِن كُلُّ مَن فِي السَّمَاوَاتِ وَالْأَرْضِ إِلَّا آتِي الرَّحْمَٰنِ عَبْدًا – لَّقَدْ أَحْصَاهُمْ وَعَدَّهُمْ عَدًّا – وَكُلُّهُمْ آتِيهِ يَوْمَ الْقِيَامَةِ فَرْدًا

*"And they say: 'The Beneficient (Allah) has begotten children.'
Indeed you have brought forth a terrible thing. Whereby almost the*

heavens are torn and the earth is split assunder and the mountains fall in ruins. That you ascribed children to the Beneficient (Allah). But it is not suitable for (the Majesty of) the Beneficient (Allah) that He should beget children. There is none in the heavens and the earth but comes unto the Beneficient (Allah) as a slave. Verily He knows their number and has counted them a full counting. And everyone of them will come to Him alone, on the Day of Resurrection."

[Mariyam:88 - 95]

Describing the Prophets with *Al-'Uboodiyah*

Concerning 'Eesa (AS) (Jesus), to whom the divinity and sonship to the deity were falsely ascribed, Allah (swt) said,

$$إِنْ هُوَ إِلَّا عَبْدٌ أَنْعَمْنَا عَلَيْهِ وَجَعَلْنَاهُ مَثَلًا لِّبَنِي إِسْرَائِيلَ$$

"He ('Eesa) was no more ~han a 'Abd. We granted Our Favour to him, and We made him an example to the Children of Israel."
[Az-Zukhruf:59]

This is why the Prophet Muhammad (saw) said in the authentic Hadeeth, "Do not flatter me as the Christians have flattered 'Eesa, son of Mariyam, for I am only a 'Abd of Allah; therefore say: 'Abd-u- Allah (the worshiper of Allah) Wa Rasool-u-hu (and His Messenger)." [1]

---

[1] Al-Bukhari narrated it in his book "Al-Jaami' As-Saheeh" upon 'Umar bin Al-Khattab(RAA).

Attributing *Al-'Uboodiyah* to the Prophet (saw) in his most perfect states

Allah (swt) further attributed *Al-'Uboodiyah* to him (saw) in his most perfect states; He (swt) said concerning Al-Israa (the Night Journey),

سُبْحَانَ الَّذِي أَسْرَىٰ بِعَبْدِهِ لَيْلًا مِّنَ الْمَسْجِدِ الْحَرَامِ إِلَى الْمَسْجِدِ الْأَقْصَى الَّذِي بَارَكْنَا حَوْلَهُ لِنُرِيَهُ مِنْ آيَاتِنَا ۚ إِنَّهُ هُوَ السَّمِيعُ الْبَصِيرُ

"Glorified be He (Allah) Who took His 'Abd (Muhammad saw) for a journey by night from the Sacred Masjid (of Makkah) to the Farthest Masjid (in Jerusalem), the neighbourhood whereof We have blessed that We might show him (Muhammad saw) of Our Signs. Verily He (Allah) is the All Hearer, the All- Seer." [Al-Israa (Bani Israa-eel):1]

And He (swt) said concerning the conveyance of revelation,

فَأَوْحَىٰ إِلَىٰ عَبْدِهِ مَا أَوْحَىٰ

"So did (Jibreel) reveal to His (Allah's) 'Abd what has been revealed (then)."

[An-Najm: 10]

Also concerning the *Da'wah* (invitation to Islam), He (swt) said.

وَأَنَّهُ لَمَّا قَامَ عَبْدُ اللَّهِ يَدْعُوهُ كَادُوا يَكُونُونَ عَلَيْهِ لِبَدًا

*"And when 'Abd-u-Allah (the worshiper of Allah; Muhammad saw)
stood up, calling unto Him (Allah Alone) they gathered against him
(saw) and almost suppressed him."*   [Al-Jinn:19]

And regarding the challenge (to those who doubted the
Prophet's (saw) mission), He (swt) said.

وَإِن كُنتُمْ فِي رَيْبٍ مِّمَّا نَزَّلْنَا عَلَىٰ عَبْدِنَا فَأْتُوا بِسُورَةٍ مِّن مِّثْلِهِ وَادْعُوا شُهَدَاءَكُم
مِّن دُونِ اللَّهِ إِن كُنتُمْ صَادِقِينَ

*"And if you are ln doubt concerning that which We have sent down
to Our 'Abd (Muhammad saw), then produce a Surah (chapter of
Al-Quran) the like thereof."*   [Al-Baqarah:23]

Ad-Deen: Islam, Eemaan, & Ihsaan

Therefore, all of Ad-Deen is included in Al-'Ibaadah. Also, it has been confirmed in As-Saheeh (1) that when Jibreel (AS) came to the Prophet (saw) in the guise of a bedouin to ask him about Al-Islam, he (saw) said, "Al-Islam is that you testify that there is none worthy of being worshipped but Allah and that Muhammad is the Messenger of Allah, and you establish As-Salaat, pay Az-Zakaat, observe the fast of Ramadhaan, and perform the Pilgrimage to the House if you are able to bear the journey."

He (Jibreel) said, "What is then Al-Eemaan?" Rasool Allah (saw) replied, "That you affirm your faith in Allah, in His Angels, in His Books, in His Messengers, in the Day of Judgement, and you affirm your faith in the Divine Decree to good and evil.

He (Jibreel) said, "What is then Al-Ihsaan?" Rasool Allah (saw) replied, "That you worship Allah as if you see Him, for though you do not see Him, verily, He sees you."

Rasool-Allah (saw) remarked at the end of the Hadeeth, "This was Jibreel. He came to instruct you in your Deen."[2] Thus, he (saw) made all of this part of Ad-Deen.

---

[2] "Al-Jaami'As-Saheeh" of Imaam Muslim bin Al-Hajjaaj

Ad-Deen includes submission and humility

Ad-Deen includes submission and humility. Subjecting a person to "Deen" means (in Arabic) that he was humbled and then became filled with humility. When it is said that somebody "Yadeen" Allah (swt) or "Yadeen" for Allah (swt), it means to "owe allegiance" to Him (awj), that is, to worship Allah (awj), obey Him, and submit to Him. Therefore, Deen-u-Allah is the worship of Him (awj), obedience to Him, and the submission to Him (swt).

Al-'Ibaadah in its original meaning is: being subdued; as a rough road is made smooth after paving.

The Levels of Love

Al-'Ibaadah which we are commanded to perform includes the meaning of humility and love, it contains extreme humility before Allah (swt) together with the extreme love for Him (awj). The uppermost level of love is the extreme adoration (Tatayum) and its lowermost level is the interest, because the heart is first interested in the beloved. After the interest comes the affection, then the love, and finally the extreme adoration. In Arabic "Taym-u-Allah" (the adorer of Allah) is used to mean "Abd-u-Allah" (the worshiper of Allah) because the adorer is the one who yields completely to his lover.

One who submits to someone with hatred is not worshipping him. And one who loves someone without submitting to him is likewise not worshiping him; this is like a man who loves his son and friends.

Therefore, neither love nor submission alone are sufficient in worshipping Allah (swt). Allah (awj) must be loved most by Al-'Abd and He (swt) must be the greatest of all in his sight. Nothing deserves complete love and submission except Allah (awj). It is a futile love when anything has been loved for other than the sake of Allah (swt). And whatever has been highly regarded without it being by the Command of Allah, its glorification is rejected.

The love for Allah (SWT) and Ar-Rasool (saw) should override any other love.

Allah (swt) said.

قُل إِن كَانَ آبَاؤُكُمْ وَأَبْنَاؤُكُمْ وَإِخْوَانُكُمْ وَأَزْوَاجُكُمْ وَعَشِيرَتُكُمْ وَأَمْوَالٌ اقْتَرَفْتُمُوهَا وَتِجَارَةٌ تَخْشَوْنَ كَسَادَهَا وَمَسَاكِنُ تَرْضَوْنَهَا أَحَبَّ إِلَيْكُم مِّنَ اللَّهِ وَرَسُولِهِ وَجِهَادٍ فِي سَبِيلِهِ فَتَرَبَّصُوا حَتَّىٰ يَأْتِيَ اللَّهُ بِأَمْرِهِ ۗ وَاللَّهُ لَا يَهْدِي الْقَوْمَ الْفَاسِقِينَ

"Say: If your fathers, your sons, your brothers, your wives, your kindred, the wealth that you have gained, the commerce in which you fear a decline, and the dwellings in which you delight are dearer to you than Allah and His Messenger, and striving hard and Fighting in His Cause; then wait until Allah brings about His Decision (torment). And Allah guides not the rebellious folk."

[At-Tawbah:24]

Thus, the essence of love should be due to Allah and His Messenger, so too with the obedience. For the obedience is due to Allah (awj) and His Messenger, and pleasing is due to Allah and His Messenger,

وَاللَّهُ وَرَسُولُهُ أَحَقُّ أَن يُرْضُوهُ إِن كَانُوا مُؤْمِنِينَ

"But it is more fitting that they should please Allah and His Messenger (Muhammad saw) if they are (true) believers." [At-

Tawbah:62]

Also, (contentment with) the provision (from Allah and His Messenger) is due to Allah (awj) and His Messenger (saw):

وَلَوْ أَنَّهُمْ رَضُوا مَا آتَاهُمُ اللَّهُ وَرَسُولُهُ

"If only they had been contented with what Allah and His Messenger (Muhammad saw) gave them."   [At-Tawbah:59]

As for Al-'Ibaadah and that which relates to it, such as reliance, fear, etc., they should not be to any except to Allah (swt) Alone. Allah (swt) said.

قُلْ يَا أَهْلَ الْكِتَابِ تَعَالَوْا إِلَىٰ كَلِمَةٍ سَوَاءٍ بَيْنَنَا وَبَيْنَكُمْ أَلَّا نَعْبُدَ إِلَّا اللَّهَ وَلَا نُشْرِكَ بِهِ شَيْئًا وَلَا يَتَّخِذَ بَعْضُنَا بَعْضًا أَرْبَابًا مِّن دُونِ اللَّهِ ۚ فَإِن تَوَلَّوْا فَقُولُوا اشْهَدُوا بِأَنَّا مُسْلِمُونَ

"Say: O people of the Scripture (Jews and Christians): 'Come to a word common to you and us that we worship none but Allah, and that we associate nothing in worship with Him, and that none of us shall take others as lords besides Allah.' Then if they turn away, say: 'Bear witness that we are Muslims.'"

[Aal 'Imraan:64]

Allah (swt) said,

وَلَوْ أَنَّهُمْ رَضُوا مَا آتَاهُمُ اللَّهُ وَرَسُولُهُ وَقَالُوا حَسْبُنَا اللَّهُ سَيُؤْتِينَا اللَّهُ مِن فَضْلِهِ وَرَسُولُهُ إِنَّا إِلَى اللَّهِ رَاغِبُونَ

"If only they had been contented with what Allah and His Messenger (Muhammad saw) gave them and had said: 'Allah is Sufficient for us. Allah and His Messenger will give us of His Bounty. We implore Allah (to enrich us)."

[At-Tawbah:59]

The rights due to Allah (awj) and to His Rasool (saw)

Thus the distribution of provision is the right of Allah and His Messenger as He (awj) said.

وَمَا آتَاكُمُ الرَّسُولُ فَخُذُوهُ وَمَا نَهَاكُمْ عَنْهُ فَانتَهُوا ۚ وَاتَّقُوا اللَّهَ ۖ إِنَّ اللَّهَ شَدِيدُ الْعِقَابِ

"And whatsoever the Messenger provides you with, take it, and whatsoever he forbids you from, abstain (from it) and fear Allah. Verily Allah is severe in punishment." [Al-Hashr:7]

Allah (awj) is Sufficient for the believers

As for the sufficer, it is Allah (swt) alone, as He (awj) says.

الَّذِينَ قَالَ لَهُمُ النَّاسُ إِنَّ النَّاسَ قَدْ جَمَعُوا لَكُمْ فَاخْشَوْهُمْ فَزَادَهُمْ إِيمَانًا وَقَالُوا حَسْبُنَا اللَّهُ وَنِعْمَ الْوَكِيلُ

"Those unto whom men said: 'Verily, the people have gathered against you (a great army) therefore fear them.' But it (only) increased them in Faith. And they said: 'For us Allah is sufficient, and He is the Best Disposer (for us).'"

[Aal 'Imraan: 173];

and

يَا أَيُّهَا النَّبِيُّ حَسْبُكَ اللَّهُ وَمَنِ اتَّبَعَكَ مِنَ الْمُؤْمِنِينَ

"O Prophet (Muhammad saw)! Sufficient for you is Allah and (also for) those who follow you of the believers." [Al-Anfaal:64]

That is, sufficient for you (Muhammad) and sufficient for those believers who followed you is Allah (awj). Whoever thought that the meaning is: Allah and the believers together are sufficient for Muhammad (saw), is surely making a tremendous error. We explained this in a different book[3].

---

[3] See Ibn Taymiyah's Minhaaj As-Sunnah, Vol. 4, p. 55, first edition, for his

All the creatures are Ibaad of Allah

Also, Allah (swt) said,

أَلَيْسَ اللَّهُ بِكَافٍ عَبْدَهُ

Is not Allah Sufficient for His 'Abd? [Az Zumar:36]

The meaning of this is that the term 'Abd refers to the one who has been subdued by Allah (awj) so that He (swt) humbled, administered, and managed him.

In this respect all creatures are actually 'Ibaad (pl. of 'Abd) of Allah (swt) -- the upright as well as the impudent, the believers and the unbelievers, the Heaven-dwellers and the Hell-dwellers -- for He (awj) is the Lord of them all and their Owner. They cannot deviate from His Will, His Omnipotence, and His Perfect Words, for no man, upright or impudent, can violate Them. Whatever He (awj) willed will be, even though they

---

refutation of those who believe that verse 64 of Surat Al-Anfaal was revealed in reference to Alee bin Abee Taalib (RAA). They claim that Allah (swt) and Alee (RAA) are sufficient for Muhammad (saw). However, Ibn Taymiyah clearly proved that according to Al-Quran and As-Sunnah one must believe that only Allah (awj) is sufficient for Muhammad (saw) and for all the creatures, otherwise one cannot escape *Kufr*.

might have not willed that. And whatever they willed will not be, unless He (swt) has already willed it. As Allah (swt) says:

$$\text{أَفَغَيْرَ دِينِ اللَّهِ يَبْغُونَ وَلَهُ أَسْلَمَ مَن فِي السَّمَاوَاتِ وَالْأَرْضِ طَوْعًا وَكَرْهًا وَإِلَيْهِ يُرْجَعُونَ}$$

Do they seek other than Deen-u-Allah? -- While all that is in the heavens and the earth have surrendered to Him willingly or unwillingly. And to Him shall all be returned.   [Aal 'Imraan:83]

Knowing the Truth

Verily, He (swt) is the Lord of all beings, their Creator, the Provider of their livelihood, the One bestowing life unto them and the One causing death to them, the fluctuator of their hearts, the disposer of their affairs. There is no lord for them but He (awj), no owner, no creator for them except He (awj) whether they admit it or deny it, and whether they recognize it or they are ignorant of it. But the faithful believers recognize it and believe in it. Unlike the one who is ignorant about it, or denies it and is arrogant towards his Lord, neither admitting nor submitting to Him (swt), although he knows that Allah (awj) is his Lord and His Creator.

For knowing the truth but being too arrogant to accept it and furthermore to then deny it, is a great torment to man, as (swt) said,

وَجَحَدُوا بِهَا وَاسْتَيْقَنَتْهَا أَنفُسُهُمْ ظُلْمًا وَعُلُوًّا ۚ فَانظُرْ كَيْفَ كَانَ عَاقِبَةُ الْمُفْسِدِينَ

And they denied them (Allah's signs) unjustly and arrogantly, though their souls were convinced thereof. So see what was the end of the mischief makers.

[An-Naml:14];

and (swt) said,

الَّذِينَ آتَيْنَاهُمُ الْكِتَابَ يَعْرِفُونَهُ كَمَا يَعْرِفُونَ أَبْنَاءَهُمْ ۖ وَإِنَّ فَرِيقًا مِّنْهُمْ لَيَكْتُمُونَ الْحَقَّ وَهُمْ يَعْلَمُونَ

Those to whom We gave the Scripture (Jews and Christians) recognize him (Muhammad saw) as they recognize their sons. But verily, a party of them knowingly conceal the truth (i.e. the attributes of Muhammad saw which are written in the Torah and Gospel).
[Al-Baqarah: 146];

and (swt) said,

قَدْ نَعْلَمُ إِنَّهُ لَيَحْزُنُكَ الَّذِي يَقُولُونَ ۖ فَإِنَّهُمْ لَا يُكَذِّبُونَكَ وَلَٰكِنَّ الظَّالِمِينَ بِآيَاتِ اللَّهِ يَجْحَدُونَ

It is not you (Muhammad saw) that they deny, but it is the Signs of Allah that the transgressors deny.　　　　　[Al An'aam:33]

The *'Uboodiyah* that is due to the Lordship of Allah (awj)

Therefore, if Al-'Abd knew that Allah (awj) is his Lord and his Creator, and that he is poor without Him and in need of Him (awj), then he would recognize *Al-'Uboodiyah* due to the Lordship of Allah. Such an 'Abd would ask of his Lord, beseech Him and rely on Him (awj). Nevertheless, he still might obey His Command or he might disobey It, and he still might worship Him (awj) and might worship Ash- Shaitaan (Satan) and idols. This type of *Al-'Uboodiyah* allows for no distinction between that of the Heaven-dwellers and that of the Hell-dwellers. With this type of *Al-'Uboodiyah* a man does not become a believer, as (swt) said,

وَمَا يُؤْمِنُ أَكْثَرُهُم بِاللَّهِ إِلَّا وَهُم مُّشْرِكُونَ

And most of them believe not in Allah except that they attribute partners (unto Him). [Yoosuf: 106]

Indeed, those pagans (of Arabia) used to admit that Allah (awj) is their Creator while worshipping other than Him. Allah (swt) said,

وَلَئِن سَأَلْتَهُم مَّنْ خَلَقَ السَّمَاوَاتِ وَالْأَرْضَ لَيَقُولُنَّ اللَّهُ

And verily, if you ask them: 'Who created the heavens and the earth?' Surely they will say: 'Allah' (has created them). [Az-Zumar:38];

and

قُل لِّمَنِ الْأَرْضُ وَمَن فِيهَا إِن كُنتُمْ تَعْلَمُونَ – سَيَقُولُونَ لِلَّهِ ۚ قُلْ أَفَلَا
تَذَكَّرُونَ – قُلْ مَن رَّبُّ السَّمَاوَاتِ السَّبْعِ وَرَبُّ الْعَرْشِ الْعَظِيمِ – سَيَقُولُونَ
لِلَّهِ ۚ قُلْ أَفَلَا تَتَّقُونَ – قُلْ مَن بِيَدِهِ مَلَكُوتُ كُلِّ شَيْءٍ وَهُوَ يُجِيرُ وَلَا يُجَارُ
عَلَيْهِ إِن كُنتُمْ تَعْلَمُونَ – سَيَقُولُونَ لِلَّهِ ۚ قُلْ فَأَنَّىٰ تُسْحَرُونَ

*Say: 'Whose is the earth and whosoever is therein? If you know!' They
will say, 'To Allah!' Say: 'Will you not then remember?' Say: 'Who
is the Lord of the seven heavens, and the Lord of the Great Throne?'
They will say, '(That belongs) to Allah,' Say: 'Will you not then fear
Allah.' Say: 'In Whose Hand is the sovereignty of everything and He
protects (all), while against Him there is no protector if you know?'
They will say, '(It belongs) to Allah,' Say: 'How then are you
bewitched (deny the truth)?'* [Al-Moo-minoon: 84-89]

The reality of *Al-'Uboodiyah*

Most of those who speak about The Truth and witness it do not witness except this very truth, the universal truth, in which the believer and the disbeliever, the upright and the impudent, are common and they witness it together. Even Iblees (Satan) admitted this truth, as well as did the Hell dwellers. Iblees said:

قَالَ رَبِّ فَأَنظِرْنِي إِلَىٰ يَوْمِ يُبْعَثُونَ

My Lord! Give me then respite till the Day they (the dead) are resurrected.

[Saad:79]

and he also said:

قَالَ رَبِّ بِمَا أَغْوَيْتَنِي لَأُزَيِّنَنَّ لَهُمْ فِي الْأَرْضِ وَلَأُغْوِيَنَّهُمْ أَجْمَعِينَ

O my Lord! Because You misled me I shall indeed adorn the path of error for them (mankind) on earth and I shall mislead them all.
[Al-Hijr 39];

and

قَالَ فَبِعِزَّتِكَ لَأُغْوِيَنَّهُمْ أَجْمَعِينَ

By Your Might then I will surely mislead them all,   [Saad:82];

and

قَالَ أَرَأَيْتَكَ هٰذَا الَّذِي كَرَّمْتَ عَلَيَّ لَئِنْ أَخَّرْتَنِ إِلَىٰ يَوْمِ الْقِيَامَةِ لَأَحْتَنِكَنَّ ذُرِّيَّتَهُ إِلَّا قَلِيلًا

Do You see this one whom You have honored above me, if You respite me (keep me alive) to the Day of Resurrection, I will surely cut the roots of his offspring (by sending them astray), all but a few!

[Al- Israa:62]

Iblees and the Hell-dwellers admit the universal truth.

And there are many similar addresses where he (Iblees) confesses that Allah (swt) is his Lord and his Creator and the Creator of all others. Similarly, the dwellers of the Hellfire will have said:

قَالُوا رَبَّنَا غَلَبَتْ عَلَيْنَا شِقْوَتُنَا وَكُنَّا قَوْمًا ضَالِّينَ

They will say: 'Our Lord! Our misfortune overwhelmed us and we were (an) erring people.'   [Al-Moo- minoon:106];

and (swt) said:

وَلَوْ تَرَىٰ إِذْ وُقِفُوا عَلَىٰ رَبِّهِمْ ۚ قَالَ أَلَيْسَ هَٰذَا بِالْحَقِّ ۚ قَالُوا بَلَىٰ وَرَبِّنَا ۚ قَالَ فَذُوقُوا الْعَذَابَ بِمَا كُنتُمْ تَكْفُرُونَ

If you could see when they (the disbelievers) will be detained in front of their Lord! He will say: 'Is not this (Resurrection and the taking of the accounts) the truth?' They will confirm: 'Yes, by our Lord!'
[Al An'aam:30]

The difference between the universal truth and the religious truth

Thus, whoever limits himself to this (universal) truth, and just recognizing it alone, but does not establish what he was commanded to do of the religious truth - which is worshipping Him and which is related to His Deity and the obedience to His (swt) Command and the command of His Messenger - he will be of the same kind as Iblees and the Hell-dwellers. Moreover, if he thought that he is one of Allah's elite and one of the possessors of the Knowledge (of the Unseen) and the Realization (of the Truth), who believe that the legislated Command and Prohibition do not hold for them, he will then be amongst the worst rejectors of faith and the atheists.

And whosoever thought that "Al-Khidr[4] and others like him were not subjected to the Command because they have witnessed the Will," his saying is one of the worst sayings of the rejectors of (faith in) Allah and His Messenger. He will remain as such (a Kaafir) until he fulfils the second type of meaning of Al-'Abd, this is Al-'Abd who is a worshiper. He should be worshipping Allah and not worshipping other than Him -- obeying His Command and the command of His Messengers, becoming loyal to the believing pious allies of Allah (swt) and

---

[4] See Surat Al-Kahf:65 and Tafseer Ibn Katheer vol. III, p. 92

disowning His (swt) enemies.

Al-'Ibaadah which pleases Allah (swt)

This 'Ibaadah is related to the attribution of the sole deity to Allah (swt). That is why the theme of At Tawheed is: "Laa Ilaaha Illa Allah," i.e. "There is none worthy of being worshipped but Allah." This stands in contrast to those who admit to Allah's Lordship but do not worship Him (swt) or they worship some other deities alongside Him (awj). In fact, the Ilaah (deity) is that which is deified by the heart with perfect love and glorification, with exaltations and respectfulness, with fear and hope, and the like. This kind of Al-'Ibaadah is what Allah likes and approves of, and by which He described His chosen 'Ibaad, and with which He sent His Messengers.

As for the other meaning of Al-'Abd, the subdued, regardless whether one admits that (status) or denies it, it is a meaning which refers to both the believer and the non-believer.

By differentiating between these two types (of 'Abd) we can recognize the difference between the religious realities, on the one hand, and the universal realities on the other. The religious realities are embodied within Al-'Ibaadah due to Allah (swt), His Deen, and His legislated Command - the realities which are beloved and approved by Him, and whose people He (Allah) grants His Allegiance to and favors them with His Jannah (Paradise). The universal realities are those in which the believer and non- believer, the upright and impudent are common.

And whoever is satisfied with the universal realities but does not follow the religious realities, he would be amongst the followers of the cursed Iblees and the rejectors of the Lord of the Worlds. And anyone who is satisfied with them (the religious realities) in certain matters but not in others, or in a certain situation but not in another, or in a certain circumstance but not in another, his Eemaan and his allegiance to Allah (swt) will diminish as much as the religious realities have been diminished. This is a serious situation in which many erring persons were mistaken, and there were so many confused seekers (of the truth) that even amongst the great Sheikhs who claim the realization (of the truth), the Tawheed, and the knowledge, there was an enormous number who slipped due to it. No one can count their number except Allah (swt) Who knows the concealed and revealed matter.

Concerning the Divine Decree and Measure

Sheikh Abd Al-Qaader (ra)[5] had pointed to this matter, as was reported upon him. He clarified that, "Many people when they reached the subject of Al-Qadhaa (the Divine Decree) and Al-Qadar (the Divine Measure) hold back. But not me. A window has been opened in it for me. I fought the measures of the Truth by the Truth for the Truth. The (real) man is he who is in strife with Al-Qadar (the Measure), not he who conforms with Al-Qadar (the Measure)."

---

[5] He is Sheikh Abd Al-Qaader bin Musa Al-Jeelaani, the pious and absternious scholar. He died in the year 561 A.H. and to him At-Tareeqah Al-Qaaderiyah is attributed but he is ar free from all the Bida' (innovations in Ad-Deen) and the heresies of this Tareeqah.

Misconception and error of Fatalism

What has been mentioned by the Sheikh (RA) is that which Allah (swt) had commanded, and (also what) His Rasool (saw) commanded. But many people erred in it. Those who erred might witness that which has been measured for one of them as to insurrections and sins, or that which has been measured for others as to insurrections and sins, even if it is *Kufr*. They witness (or accept) that erring as occurring by the Will of Allah and by His Qadhaa and Qadar (His Decree and Measure), and as being included in the virtue of His Lordship and the requirement of His Will. They think that submitting to sin and conforming with it and accepting it, etc. is a Deen, a straight path, and an 'Ibadah. In this they are similar to the polytheists who said:

$$\text{لَوْ شَاءَ اللَّهُ مَا أَشْرَكْنَا وَلَا آبَاؤُنَا وَلَا حَرَّمْنَا مِن شَيْءٍ}$$

If Allah had willed, we would not have taken partners (in Al-'Ibaadah) with Him nor would our fathers, and we would not have forbidden anything (against His Will).   [Al-An'aam: 148];

and they said:

$$\text{أَنُطْعِمُ مَن لَّوْ يَشَاءُ اللَّهُ أَطْعَمَهُ}$$

Shall we feed those whom, if Allah willed, He (Himself) would have fed?

[Ya Seen: 47];

وَقَالُوا لَوْ شَاءَ الرَّحْمَٰنُ مَا عَبَدْنَاهُم

If it had been the Will of the Most Beneficient (Allah) we should not have worshipped them.

[Az- Zukhruf:20]

Al-Qadar which we were ordered to be patient with

If they were truly rightly guided they would know that we have been commanded to be contented with Al-Qadar (the Measure of Allah) and be patient with its injunction only in the calamities which afflict us such as poverty, sickness, and fear. Allah (swt) said:

مَا أَصَابَ مِن مُّصِيبَةٍ إِلَّا بِإِذْنِ اللَّهِ ۗ وَمَن يُؤْمِن بِاللَّهِ يَهْدِ قَلْبَهُ

No calamity can occur but with the leave of Allah, and whosoever believes in Allah, He guides his heart (aright). [At-Taghaabun:11]

Some of the righteous predecessors said about this: "It is the man who was afflicted with a calamity, but he knows it is from Allah (awj) and therefore contentedly accepted it."

Allah (swt) said:

مَا أَصَابَ مِن مُّصِيبَةٍ فِي الْأَرْضِ وَلَا فِي أَنفُسِكُمْ إِلَّا فِي كِتَابٍ مِّن قَبْلِ أَن نَّبْرَأَهَا ۚ إِنَّ ذَٰلِكَ عَلَى اللَّهِ يَسِيرٌ - لِّكَيْلَا تَأْسَوْا عَلَىٰ مَا فَاتَكُمْ وَلَا تَفْرَحُوا بِمَا آتَاكُمْ ۗ وَاللَّهُ لَا يُحِبُّ كُلَّ مُخْتَالٍ فَخُورٍ

No misfortune can happen on earth or in yourselves but it is recorded in a Scripture before We bring it forth into existence. Verily, that is easy for Allah. In order that you may not be sad over matters that you fail to get, nor rejoice because of that which has been given to you.   [Al-Hadeed:22-23]

The argument between Adam and Musa (saw)

It is reported in the Saheehein[6] upon the Prophet (saw) who said:

"Adam and Musa held a disputation. Musa said: 'You are Adam whom Allah created with His Hand, into whom He breathed by His Spirit, to whom He made the Angels prostrate, and whom He taught the names of everything, so why have you expelled us and yourself from Al-Jannah (the Paradise)?' Adam replied, 'And you are Musa whom Allah favoured with His Message and His Words, have you not found that it had been written on me before I was created?' He (Musa) said: 'Yes, indeed'" Then he (Rasool Allah saw) said: "So Adam got the better of Musa in the argument." [7]

Adam did not prove his argument against Musa by means of Al-Qadar (the Measure), thinking that the sinner can use Al-Qadar (the Measure) as an argument. Neither a Muslim nor any sane man would say that. If it were an excuse, it would be an excuse for Iblees as well as for Nooh's people, Hood's people, and every

---

[6] "Al-Jaami' As-Saheeh" of Imaam Bukhaari and "Al-Jaami' As-Saheeh" of Imaam Muslim

[7] Sheikh Al-Islaam Ibn Taymiyah detailed this subject in his book "Al-Ihtijaaj bi Al-Qadar." This book has been verified by Al-Muhaddith As-Sheikh Muhammad Naasir Ad-Deen Al Albaani

Kaafir.

Neither did Musa blame Adam for the sin itself, for Adam did repent to his Lord and was then (forgiven and) gained favour and was guided by Him (awj). But he blamed him for the calamity which afflicted them because of the sin; that is why he said to Adam, "Why did you have us and yourself expelled out of Al-Jannah (the Paradise)?" Adam thus replied, "This had been written on me before I was created."

So the action and the calamity resulting from it were pre-measured, and what has been pre-measured of calamity one should submit to. This is the complement to the acceptance of Allah as Lord.

What should the sinful do?

As for the sins, Al-'Abd should not be sinful, but if he does sin he should ask forgiveness and should repent. He should repent from the faults and should be patient with the calamities. Allah (swt) said:

فَاصْبِرْ إِنَّ وَعْدَ اللَّهِ حَقٌّ وَاسْتَغْفِرْ لِذَنبِكَ وَسَبِّحْ بِحَمْدِ رَبِّكَ بِالْعَشِيِّ وَالْإِبْكَارِ

So be patient (O Muhammad saw). Verily the Promise of Allah is true, and ask forgiveness for your fault.　　　　　[Al-Moo-min:55]

وَإِن تَصْبِرُوا وَتَتَّقُوا لَا يَضُرُّكُمْ كَيْدُهُمْ شَيْئًا

But if you remain patient and pious, not the least harm will their cunning do to you.　　　　　[Aal 'Imraan: 120];

وَإِن تَصْبِرُوا وَتَتَّقُوا فَإِنَّ ذَٰلِكَ مِنْ عَزْمِ الْأُمُورِ

But if you persevere patiently and ward off evil. Indeed, these are the things which you should hold fast to.　　　　　[Aal 'Imraan:186];

and Yoosuf (AS) said:

إِنَّهُ مَن يَتَّقِ وَيَصْبِرْ فَإِنَّ اللَّهَ لَا يُضِيعُ أَجْرَ الْمُحْسِنِينَ

Verily, he who fears Allah and is patient, then surely Allah makes not the reward of the good-doers to be lost.　　　　　[Yoosuf:90]

CHAPTER II

The Duty of Enjoining Right Conduct

As to the sins of Al-'Ibaad, Al-'Abd in the matters of sins should enjoin the right and forbid the evil with all his potential. He should make Jihaad Fee Sabeel-Ellah (struggle in the Cause of Allah awj) against the Kuffaar and the hypocrites; he should have allegiance with Allah's allies and take for an enemy Allah's (swt) enemies; and he should love for Allah and hate for Allah, as Allah (swt) said,

"O you who believe! Take not my enemies and your enemies as friends, offering them (your) love even though they have disbelieved in that truth which has come to you, and have driven out the Messenger (Muhammad saw) and yourselves (from your home-land) (only) because you believe in Allah your Lord! If you have come forth to strive in My Way and to seek My Good Pleasure (then take not these disbelievers as your friends). You show friendship to them in secret, while I am fully aware of what you conceal and what you reveal. And whosoever of you (Muslims) does that, then indeed he has gone (far) astray, (away) from the straight Path. Should they gain the upper hand over you, they would behave to you as enemies, and stretch forth their hands and their tongues against you for evil and they desire that you should disbelieve. Neither your relatives nor your children will benefit you on the Day of Resurrection (against Allah). He

will judge between you. And Allah is the All-Seer of what you
do.

Indeed there has been an excellent example for you in Ibraaheem
and those with him, when they said to their people:

إِنَّا بُرَآءُ مِنكُمْ وَمِمَّا تَعْبُدُونَ مِن دُونِ اللَّهِ كَفَرْنَا بِكُمْ وَبَدَا بَيْنَنَا وَبَيْنَكُمُ الْعَدَاوَةُ

وَالْبَغْضَاءُ أَبَدًا حَتَّىٰ تُؤْمِنُوا بِاللَّهِ وَحْدَهُ

*'Verily, we are disowning you and whatever you worship besides
Allah, we have rejected you, and there has arisen between us and
you hostility and hatred for ever, -- until you believe in Allah Alone.'*
[Al-Mumtahanah: 1-4];

and

لَّا تَجِدُ قَوْمًا يُؤْمِنُونَ بِاللَّهِ وَالْيَوْمِ الْآخِرِ يُوَادُّونَ مَنْ حَادَّ اللَّهَ وَرَسُولَهُ وَلَوْ كَانُوا

آبَاءَهُمْ أَوْ أَبْنَاءَهُمْ أَوْ إِخْوَانَهُمْ أَوْ عَشِيرَتَهُمْ ۚ أُولَٰئِكَ كَتَبَ فِي قُلُوبِهِمُ الْإِيمَانَ

وَأَيَّدَهُم بِرُوحٍ مِّنْهُ ۖ

*You will not find any people who believe in Allah and the Last Day,
making friendship with those who oppose Allah and His Messenger
(Muhammad saw) even though they were their fathers, or their sons,
or their brothers or their kindred (people). For such only He has
written Faith in their hearts and strengthened them with spirit
(proofs and guidance) from Himself.*

[Al-Mujaadalah:22];

The pious and the wrong-doers shall not be treated equally.

أَفَنَجْعَلُ الْمُسْلِمِينَ كَالْمُجْرِمِينَ

Shall We then treat the submitting Muslims the same as the criminals?

[Al-Qalam:35];

and

أَمْ نَجْعَلُ الَّذِينَ آمَنُوا وَعَمِلُوا الصَّالِحَاتِ كَالْمُفْسِدِينَ فِي الْأَرْضِ أَمْ نَجْعَلُ الْمُتَّقِينَ كَالْفُجَّارِ

Shall We treat those who believe and do good deeds as those who do mischief on earth? Or shall We treat those who ward off evil the same as the wicked? [Saad:28];

and

أَمْ حَسِبَ الَّذِينَ اجْتَرَحُوا السَّيِّئَاتِ أَن نَّجْعَلَهُمْ كَالَّذِينَ آمَنُوا وَعَمِلُوا الصَّالِحَاتِ سَوَاءً مَّحْيَاهُمْ وَمَمَاتُهُمْ ۚ سَاءَ مَا يَحْكُمُونَ

Or do those who earn evil deeds think that We shall hold them equal with those who believe and do good deeds, -- in their present life and after their death? Worst is the judgment that they make. [Al-Jaathiyah:21];

and

وَمَا يَسْتَوِي الْأَعْمَىٰ وَالْبَصِيرُ – وَلَا الظُّلُمَاتُ وَلَا النُّورُ – وَلَا الظِّلُّ وَلَا الْحَرُورُ – وَمَا يَسْتَوِي الْأَحْيَاءُ وَلَا الْأَمْوَاتُ ۚ إِنَّ اللَّهَ يُسْمِعُ مَن يَشَاءُ ۖ وَمَا أَنتَ بِمُسْمِعٍ مَّن فِي الْقُبُورِ

Not alike are the blind and the seeing. Not are (alike) the darkness and the light. Nor are (alike) the shade and the sun's full heat. Nor are (alike) the living and the dead. Verily, Allah makes whom He wills to hear, but you cannot make to hear those who are in the graves. [Faatir:19-22];

Parables from Allah (awj)

ضَرَبَ اللَّهُ مَثَلًا رَّجُلًا فِيهِ شُرَكَاءُ مُتَشَاكِسُونَ وَرَجُلًا سَلَمًا لِّرَجُلٍ هَلْ يَسْتَوِيَانِ مَثَلًا ۚ الْحَمْدُ لِلَّهِ ۚ بَلْ أَكْثَرُهُمْ لَا يَعْلَمُونَ

Allah puts forth a parable -- a (slave) man belonging to many partners (like those who worship others along with Allah) disputing with one another, and a (slave) man belonging entirely to one master, (like those who worship Allah Alone), are those two equal in comparison? [Az-Zumar:29];

and

ضَرَبَ اللَّهُ مَثَلًا عَبْدًا مَّمْلُوكًا لَّا يَقْدِرُ عَلَىٰ شَيْءٍ وَمَن رَّزَقْنَاهُ مِنَّا رِزْقًا حَسَنًا فَهُوَ يُنفِقُ مِنْهُ سِرًّا وَجَهْرًا ۚ هَلْ يَسْتَوُونَ ۚ الْحَمْدُ لِلَّهِ ۚ بَلْ أَكْثَرُهُمْ لَا يَعْلَمُونَ - وَضَرَبَ اللَّهُ مَثَلًا رَّجُلَيْنِ أَحَدُهُمَا أَبْكَمُ لَا يَقْدِرُ عَلَىٰ شَيْءٍ وَهُوَ كَلٌّ عَلَىٰ مَوْلَاهُ أَيْنَمَا يُوَجِّههُّ لَا يَأْتِ بِخَيْرٍ ۖ هَلْ يَسْتَوِي هُوَ وَمَن يَأْمُرُ بِالْعَدْلِ ۚ وَهُوَ عَلَىٰ صِرَاطٍ مُّسْتَقِيمٍ

Allah puts forward the example (of two men), one, a slave under the possession of another, he has no power of any sort, and (the other), a man on whom We have bestowed a good provision from Ourselves, and he spends thereof secretly and openly. Can they be equal? (By no means not.) Praise be to Allah. Nay! Most of them know not. And Allah puts forward (another) example of two men, one of them dumb, who has no power over anything, and he is a burden to his master, whichever way he directs him, he brings no good. Is such a man equal with one who commands justice, and is himself on a Straight Path?   [An-Nahl:75-76];

and

لَا يَسْتَوِي أَصْحَابُ النَّارِ وَأَصْحَابُ الْجَنَّةِ ۚ أَصْحَابُ الْجَنَّةِ هُمُ الْفَائِزُونَ

Not equal are the dwellers of the Fire and the companions of Paradise. It is the companions of Paradise that will be successful.
                                                      [Al-Hashr:20]

The distinction between the people of righteousness and people of falsehood

In these and similar Ayaat, Allah (swt) makes a distinction between the people of right and falsehood, the people of obedience and disobedience, the people of uprightness and licentiousness, the people of guidance and misguidance, the people of transgression and righteousness, and the people of truthfulness and deceit.

The most horrifying *Kufr*

Therefore, anyone who witnesses the universal truth without the religious truth will hold equal all these types of people whom Allah (swt) has made an ultimate distinction between. This reconciliation will eventually conduce him to even reconcile between Allah (awj) and the idols, as Allah (swt) said about this type of people.

$$\text{تَاللَّهِ إِن كُنَّا لَفِي ضَلَالٍ مُّبِينٍ - إِذْ نُسَوِّيكُم بِرَبِّ الْعَالَمِينَ}$$

By Allah, we were truly in a manifest error. When we held you (false deities) as equals (in Al-'Ibaadah) with the Lord of the Worlds.
[Ash-Shu'araa:97-98]

They eventually reach the point where they reconcile between Allah (awj) and every existing being. And they considered all that which He (awj) deserves of 'Ibaadah and obedience as being due to every existing created thing since they made His (awj) existence the same as the existence of the created things. This is of the most horrifying *Kufr* and atheism towards the Lord of all the beings. They reach by their *Kufr* the point where they do not bear witness that they are 'Ibaad-u-Allah, neither by the meaning of the subdued ones nor by the meaning of the worshipping ones. They witness that they themselves are the Truth as has been declared by their false idols, e.g. Ibn 'Arabee who wrote "Al- Fousous," and other slandering atheists such as Ibn Sab'een and his like. They even witness that they are simultaneously the worshipers and the ones being worshipped.

This, indeed, is not the witnessing of the truth, neither the universal one nor the religious one, but it is rather a going astray and blindness from witnessing the universal truth, for they made the existence of the Creator the same as that of the created. They made every good and bad quality as an attribute to both the Creator and the created, for they consider the existence of the former as being the same as the existence of the latter. But the believers in Allah (swt) and His Messengers, both commoner and elite, are the people of the Quran, as the Prophet (saw) said, "Verily, Allah has (favourite) people amongst mankind." He was asked, "Who are they? O Messenger of Allah." He replied, "The people of Al Quran, they are people of Allah and His elite." [8]

---

[8] Narrated by Ahmad and it is Hasan for it is Saheeh due to another route. See Silsilat Al-Ahaadeeth Adh-Dha'eefah No. 1582.

The *Kufr* of those who believe in the incarnation

These people know that Allah (awj) is the Lord, the Owner, and the Creator of everything. And that the Creator is different from the created being. He (swt) is neither incarnated in the being nor combined with him, nor is His (swt) existence the same as the being's existence. Indeed, the Christians were not declared by Allah (awj) as Kuffaar (unbelievers) except for that they believed in the incarnation and combination of Allah (swt) with Al-Maseeh (Jesus AS). So how about those who made this true about every creature? Yet, they know fully well that Allah (swt) ordered obedience to Him (awj) and obedience to His Messengers, and that Allah (awj) does not like corruption nor approves Al-*Kufr* for His 'Ibaad. And all the creation ought to worship Him (swt) so that they obey His commands, and ask for His aid to fulfill that; as He (awj) said in the Opening of the Scripture:

إِيَّاكَ نَعْبُدُ وَإِيَّاكَ نَسْتَعِينُ

It is You we worship and it is You we ask for help. [Al-Faatihah:5]

The Reality of Al-'Ibaadah and the obedience

As aspects of worshipping and obeying Him (swt) are the commanding of good and forbidding of evil as much as possible, and the Jihaad Fee Sabeel-Ellah (the struggle in the Cause of Allah) against the people of *Kufr* and hypocrisy. They (the believers) strive for the establishment of His Deen, seeking help from Him, lifting and removing through that as much as they can of mischiefs, pushing away thereof what could be of fearful consequences.

This is very similar to the human being who removes actual hunger by eating, and with it pushes away future hunger. Also, when it gets cold, he pushes it away by wearing extra clothing. Similarly is the case of every required need which is used to push away the harm. As they (the Companions of the Prophet) said to the Prophet (saw): "O Rasool-Allah! How about the medicines which we use to cure ourselves with, and Ruqa [9] we seek as remedies, and the safeguards we use to protect ourselves with? Do they prevent any of Allah's Qadar (Measure)?" He (saw) replied: "They are indeed aspects of Allah's Qadar (Measure)." Also, in the Hadeeth: "The supplication and the affliction confront each other and struggle in between the heaven

---

[9] Pl. of Ruqyah, recitation of Quranic verses or prescribed supplications.

and the earth." [10] This is the state of the believers in Allah (swt) and in His Messenger (saw), who offer their 'Ibaadah to Allah. All the aforementioned are aspects of 'Ibaadah. As for those who witness the universal truth -- the Lordship of Allah (swt) for everything -- and make it as an obstruction for not following His legislated religious Command, they are at different levels of being astray.

---

[10] Narrated by Imaam Ahmad in his Musnad (31421) and Ibn Maajah 3437 and also narrated by At- Tirmidthi

There can be no argument in using Al-Qadar to contradict Ash-Sharee'ah

The extravagant ones amongst them take it for absolute and general. They use Al-Qadar (the Measure) as an excuse in arguing for whatever they do in opposition to Ash-Sharee'ah (the legislated law). The saying of these people is worse than the saying of the Jews and Christians. It is of the same type as the saying of the Mushrikeen who said,

سَيَقُولُ الَّذِينَ أَشْرَكُوا لَوْ شَاءَ اللَّهُ مَا أَشْرَكْنَا وَلَا آبَاؤُنَا وَلَا حَرَّمْنَا مِن شَيْءٍ

If Allah had willed, we would not have taken partners (in Al-'Ibaadah) with Him nor would our fathers, and we would not have had forbidden anything (against His Will).   [Al-An'aam: 148]

And they said,

وَقَالُوا لَوْ شَاءَ الرَّحْمَٰنُ مَا عَبَدْنَاهُم

If it had been the Will of the Most Beneficient (Allah) we should not have worshipped *them.*   [Az Zukhruf:20]

These people are the most self-contradicting beings amongst the whole population of the earth. Rather, anyone who argues using Al-Qadar (the Measure) is self-contradicting. It is not possible to approve whatever every and each human being does. It is incumbent on him when an unjust person practices his unjustice on him, or on other people; or promotes corruption on earth; or starts shedding the blood of people; or rendering adultery allowable; or destroying the civilization and humanity; and the like of such types of harm which the people can not bear, that he should repel this fate and punish the unjust person in order to prevent his aggression and the aggression of those like him. It would be said to him: If Al-Qadar (the Measure) is an excuse in arguing, then let anybody do to you and to other people whatever he likes. If, rather, it is not an excuse in arguing, then the origin of your saying is proven false.

Using the universal truth as an excuse is not but following the whims and desires

The people of this kind of saying who use the universal truth as an excuse in arguing (for their mischiefs) do not reject it nor do they fully adhere to it. Rather, they follow their own whims and desires. Some scholars described them as: "In the instance of obedience, you have a free-will. And in the instance of disobedience you are a fatalist. Whichever discipline fits your desire you take as your discipline."

Another kind of these people (who only witness the universal truth) claim the realization of the Truth) and the possession of the Knowledge. They pretend that the commanding and forbidding ought to be only for him who witnesses for himself certain deeds and confirms for himself certain attributes. But he who witnesses that his deeds are created, or that he is being forced to perform them, and Allah is the one who directs him as He directs all other moving things, the promise and threat are removed from upon him.

Man freely chooses his own deeds and the legislated commandment cannot be forfeited

They might say, "Whoever witnesses the Will, the legislated commandment has been dropped from upon him." They alleged that Al-Khidr has had the legislated commandment removed from upon him since he witnessed the Will.

These people differentiate between the populace and the elite who witnessed the universal truth -- they witnessed that Allah is the creator of the creatures' actions and that He conforms and directs all beings.

Some other times they differentiate between the person who knows that in cognizance and the person who experiences that by witnessing. They do not drop off the legislated commandment from the person who only believes in that and just acknowledges it. But they drop it off of who witnesses it; the one who sees no action for himself to begin with.

As such, these people take fatalism and the affirmation of Al-Qadar (the Measure) as the waiver from being commanded.

In this, many sects which are affiliated with the Realization, the Cognizance, and the Unification have fallen. The reason behind that is: they were too narrow-minded to imagine that Al-'Abd can be commanded with something contradicting what has been measured for him. Such was the case of Al Mu'tazilah and the rest of the Qadariyah (people of free-will) who were too narrow-minded to grasp this fact.

Thus, Al-Mu'tazilah affirmed the legislated Commanding and Forbidding but did not do so with Al- Qadhaa and Al-Qadar (the Decree and the Measure), which are the General Will of Allah (swt) and His Creation of Al-'Ibaad's deeds.

Commanding and forbidding is not only imposed on the unenlightened people

On the other hand, the people (of Realization, Knowledge, and Unification) affirmed Al-Qadhaa and Al-Qadar (the Decree and the Measure) but rejected the Commanding and Forbidding for those who witnessed Al-Qadar, for they could not reject it in its totality (i.e for all the people). The saying of these latter is worse than the saying of Al-Mu'tazilah. That is why there were no such people amongst the predecessors of this Ummah. They categorize the Commanding and Forbidding solely for the so-called unenlightened people who did not witness the universal truth. That is why they drop off the Commanding and Forbidding from upon him who attains the witnessing of this truth and they say: He becomes of the elite. Furthermore, they might misinterpret for this purpose the saying of Allah (awj),

وَاعْبُدْ رَبَّكَ حَتَّىٰ يَأْتِيَكَ الْيَقِينُ

And worship your Lord until there comes unto you the Hour that is certain (i.e. death). [Al-Hijr:99]

According to them the certainty is the knowledge of this Reality.

Commanding good & forbidding evil shall not be forfeited until death

The saying of these people is a clear *Kufr* -- although some sects fell into this without knowing that it is *Kufr*. For it is known, by necessity, from the Deen of Islam that the Commanding and Forbidding are incumbent on every 'Abd as long as he is sane until he dies. They would not be waivered for him by his witnessing Al-Qadar nor by other means. Hence, whoever did not know that, it should be made known to him. If he insisted on believing in the wavering of the Commanding and Forbidding, he should be killed.

Such utterances were numerous amongst the recent people. Whereas amongst the predecessors of this Ummah such utterances were not known. For these utterances are indeed in opposition to Allah (swt) and His Messenger (saw), hostile to Them, an obstruction in His path, renouncing Him, denial of His Messengers, antagonistic to Him in His Decree even though the one who says that might not be aware of it and believes that what he is on is the way of the Messenger (saw) and the way of the enlightened allies (Awleyaa) of Allah.

In such a way he is similar to the one who believes that As-Salaat is not incumbent on him since he can dispense with it because of the experiences of the hearts which have occurred to him; or believes that liquors are allowable to him due to him being of the elite who could not be harmed by drinking liquors; or that lusting is allowable for him because he became as a sea which can not be spoiled by sins, etc.

Making Bid'ah and/or using Al-Qadar as an argument is resemblance to All-Mushrikeen

There is no doubt that Al-Mushrikeen who denied Ar Rasool (saw) fluctuated between Al-Bid'ah (the innovation in Ad-Deen) which opposes the legislation of Allah (swt), and using Al-Qadar for argument to oppose the Command of Allah (awj). Thus, the aforementioned types of people have resemblance to the Mushrikeen; they either make Bid'ah, or use Al Qadar for argument, or combine the two matters as Allah (swt) has said about Al-Mushrikeen,

When they commit a disgraceful sin, they say: 'We found our fathers doing it, and Allah has commanded us to do so.' Say: 'Nay, Allah never commands what is disgraceful. Do you say of Allah what you know not?' [Al-A'raaf:29], and as He (awj) has also said concerning them,

سَيَقُولُ الَّذِينَ أَشْرَكُوا لَوْ شَاءَ اللَّهُ مَا أَشْرَكْنَا وَلَا آبَاؤُنَا وَلَا حَرَّمْنَا مِن شَيْءٍ

Those who take partners (in Al-'Ibaadah) with Allah will say:'If Allah had willed, we would not have taken partners (in Al-'Ibaadah) with Him nor would our fathers, and we would not have had forbidden anything (against His will).' [Al-An'aam: 148]

Legalizing the forbidden and blindly following the forefathers

And He (swt) has mentioned regarding Al Mushrikeen and what they have innovated in Ad -Deen such as legalizing Al-Haraam, and worshipping Allah with something He (swt) did not legislate, as in His (swt) saying,

And according to their pretending, they say that such and such cattle and crops are forbidden, and none should eat of them except those whom we allow. And there are cattle forbidden to use for burden or any other work and cattle on which (at slaughtering) the Name of Allah is not pronounced: - inventions against Him (Allah). [Al-An'aam:138] - until the end of the Surah. Also, as in Surat Al-A'raaf, His (swt) saying,

O Children of Adam! Let not Ash-Shaitaan (Satan) deceive you, likewise as he got your parents out of Al-Jannah,... up to His (swt) saying,

When they commit a disgraceful sin, they say: 'We found our fathers doing it, and Allah has commanded us to do so.' Say: 'Nay, Allah never commands what is disgraceful. Do you say of Allah what you know not?' Say (O Muhammad saw): 'My Lord has commanded justice and (said) that you should face only your Lord (Allah) in each and every prostration (i.e. prayer, and not to face other false deities and idols) and invoke Him only,

making your Deen sincere to Him by not joining in 'Ibaadah any partner to Him and with the intention that you are doing your deeds for Allah's Sake only.'
- up to His (swt) saying,

And eat and drink but waste not by extravagance. Certainly He (Allah) likes not the extravangants. Say (O Muhammad saw): 'Who has forbidden the adoration with clothes given by Allah which He has produced for His 'Ibaad and the delightful legal things of food?' Up to His (swt) saying,

The things that Allah (swt) has forbidden are the blatant sins

Say (O Muhammad saw):

قُلْ إِنَّمَا حَرَّمَ رَبِّيَ الْفَوَاحِشَ مَا ظَهَرَ مِنْهَا وَمَا بَطَنَ وَالْإِثْمَ وَالْبَغْيَ بِغَيْرِ الْحَقِّ وَأَن تُشْرِكُوا بِاللَّهِ مَا لَمْ يُنَزِّلْ بِهِ سُلْطَانًا وَأَن تَقُولُوا عَلَى اللَّهِ مَا لَا تَعْلَمُونَ

'But the things that my Lord has forbidden are the blatant sins whether committed openly or secretly, sins (of all kinds), unrighteous oppression, to join partners (in Al 'Ibaadah) with Allah for which He has given no authority, and saying things about Allah of which you have no knowledge.'　　　　　[Al-A'raaf:26-32]

These people may call what they have innovated of Bida': Truth, as they do call what they realize of Al Qadar: Truth. The path of the Truth according to them is the conduct of he who does not confine himself to the Legislator's Commandment nor His Prohibition; rather, it is the path of whatever he sees, tastes, and finds in his heart inspite of what is in it of heedlessness for Allah (awj), etc.

These people do not consistently use Al-Qadar for argument. Rather, their basis is to follow their own opinions and desires and make what they see and what they desire the truth. Thus they command the people to follow this but not the Command of Allah (awj) and His Messenger (saw). This is similar to the

Bida' of the scholastics such as Al Jahamiyah and others who make their innovated sayings, which are opposing the Scripture and the Sunnah, rational realities which must be believed and not that which has been audibly transmitted (Quran and Sunnah). As for the Scripture and the Sunnah, they either twist the text out of its proper context or they totally neglect it. They do not mediate the text properly nor do they comprehend it. Rather, they say: We refer its meaning to Allah, inspite of their belief in the adverse of its meaning.

Reality is not what man states and feels

If these people were confronted with what they claim, i.e. opposing rationalities to the Scripture and the Sunnah, you will find heresies and corrupt beliefs. As well, if they were confronted with what they claim of realities pertaining to the Awliyaa (allies of Allah) and which are opposing the Scripture and the Sunnah, you will find vain desires which can only be followed by the enemies of Allah and not His allies.

The origin of the misguidance of anyone who went astray is in putting forward his rationale and not the text revealed by Allah, and putting forward the following of desire and not the following of Allah's Commandment. For taste and passion are relative to what Al-'Abd loves and desires. Every lover has a certain taste and passion according to his love and his desire.

The sweetness of Al-Eemaan

Thus, the people of Eemaan have of taste and passion which is in line with what the Prophet (saw) has shown in his authentic Hadeeth, "There are three qualities of which he who is characterized by them will taste the sweetness of Al-Eemaan: he to whom Allah and His Messenger are dearer than all else; he who loves a human being naught but for the sake of Allah alone; and he who has as great abhorrence of returning to *Kufr* after Allah has rescued him from it, as he has of being cast into Hell."[11]

Also he (saw) said in an authentic Hadeeth, "He who has tasted the savour of Al-Eemaan is he who is well-pleased with Allah as Lord, with Al-Islam as Deen, and with Muhammad as a Prophet." [12]

---

[11] Narrated by Al-Bukhaari and Muslim upon Anas bin Maalik (RM)

[12] Narrated by Muslim upon Al-'Abbaas bin 'Abd Al-Muttalib (RAA)

Following the lusts and desires is nothing but taking rivals to Allah (awj)

As for those people of *Kufr*, Bida', and lusts: everyone has his own subjectivity.

It was said to Sufyaan bin 'Uyaynah, "What happened to the people of desires so that they have an extreme passion for their desires." He replied, "Did you forget the saying of Allah (swt):

And their hearts absorbed (the 'Ibaadah of) the Calf. ?[Al-Baqarah:93] Ibn 'Uyaynah said this or something similar to it.

Thus the worshipers of the idols love their deities as Allah (swt) said,

$$وَمِنَ النَّاسِ مَن يَتَّخِذُ مِن دُونِ اللَّهِ أَندَادًا يُحِبُّونَهُمْ كَحُبِّ اللَّهِ ۖ وَالَّذِينَ آمَنُوا أَشَدُّ حُبًّا لِّلَّهِ$$

And of mankind are some who take (for 'Ibaadah) others besides Allah as rivals (to Allah). They love them as they love Allah. But those who believe love Allah more (than anything else). [Al-Baqarah:165];

and He (awj) said.

فَإِن لَّمْ يَسْتَجِيبُوا لَكَ فَاعْلَمْ أَنَّمَا يَتَّبِعُونَ أَهْوَاءَهُمْ ۚ وَمَنْ أَضَلُّ مِمَّنِ اتَّبَعَ هَوَاهُ بِغَيْرِ هُدًى مِّنَ اللَّهِ ۚ إِنَّ اللَّهَ لَا يَهْدِي الْقَوْمَ الظَّالِمِينَ

But if they answer you not (i.e. do not believe in your doctrine nor follow you) then know that they only follow their own lusts. And who is more astray than one who follows his own lusts without guidance from Allah? [Al-Qasas:50];

and He (swt) also said

إِن يَتَّبِعُونَ إِلَّا الظَّنَّ وَمَا تَهْوَى الْأَنفُسُ ۖ وَلَقَدْ جَاءَهُم مِّن رَّبِّهِمُ الْهُدَىٰ

They follow but a guess and that which their souls desire. And indeed there has already come to them the Guidance from their Lord! [Najm:23]

The absolute love is common amongst the believers and non-believers

That is why these people deviate; they become very fond of listening to the poetry and the sounds which stimulate the general love which is not specific to the people of Eemaan. It is the rather common love found amongst the lover of the Beneficient, the lover of the idols, the lover of the crosses, the lover of the nations, the lover of the brethren, the lover of the beardless men, and the lover of women. And these are the ones who follow their own tastes and passions without any account, in doing so, of the Scripture, the Sunnah, or the way the righteous predecessors were on.

The one who opposes that with which Allah (awj) had sent His Messenger as to worshipping Him Alone, obeying Him and obeying His Messenger is never following any Deen which has been legislated by Allah (awj) as He (swt) said,

ثُمَّ جَعَلْنَاكَ عَلَىٰ شَرِيعَةٍ مِّنَ الْأَمْرِ فَاتَّبِعْهَا وَلَا تَتَّبِعْ أَهْوَاءَ الَّذِينَ لَا يَعْلَمُونَ – إِنَّهُمْ لَن يُغْنُوا عَنكَ مِنَ اللَّهِ شَيْئًا ۚ وَإِنَّ الظَّالِمِينَ بَعْضُهُمْ أَوْلِيَاءُ بَعْضٍ ۖ وَاللَّهُ وَلِيُّ الْمُتَّقِينَ

Then We have put you (O Muhammad saw) on the (right) Way (i.e. Islamic Legislation). So follow that (Islamic Legislation), and follow not the desires of those who know not. Verily, the wrong-doers

are protectors to one another, but Allah is the Protector of the pious (who fear Him and avoid evil).

[Al Jaathiyah:18-19]

He is rather following his own desire without any guidance from Allah. Allah (swt) said,

أَمْ لَهُمْ شُرَكَاءُ شَرَعُوا لَهُم مِّنَ الدِّينِ مَا لَمْ يَأْذَن بِهِ اللَّهُ

Or do they have partners with Allah who have legislated for them of the Deen's matters that which Allah allowed not?   [Ash-Shoora:21]

In this, they are sometimes involved in a Bid'ah which they call: Truth. They put this ahead of that which Allah has legislated; and some other times they use the universal Measure against the Sharee'ah as Allah had stated about Al-Mushrikeen as mentioned above.

The commanded means are aspects of Al-'Ibaadah

Amongst these is a group held in highest regard by these people. These hold fast to what they have chosen by their own desires of the well-known duties, and they avoid the well-known prohibitions. Yet, they go astray by leaving that which they were commanded with as to the means, which are themselves aspects of Al-'Ibaadah, thinking that the one who witnessed Al-Qadar (the Measure) would abandon that. Such is the one amongst them who considers the reliance (on Allah) or considers the supplication as being for the populace's level and not being for the elite's, based on that whoever witnessed Al-Qadar (the Measure) would know that what has been measured shall be; thus, there will be no need for that. This is a manifest misguidance.

Allah (swt) measured the effects by their causes, as He (awj) measured happiness and misfortune by their causes. The Prophet (saw) said, "For Allah has created some people to go to Al-Jannah. He created it for them when they were still in their fathers' loins, and they shall do in compliance with Al- Jannah's dwellers. And He created others for An Naar. He created it for them when they were still in their fathers' loins, and they shall do in compliance with An-Naar's dwellers." [13]

---

[13] Narrated by Ahmad, Muslim, and Abu Dawud.

Also, when the Prophet (saw) told them (the companions), "Allah has recorded the Measures," they said, "O Rasool-Allah! Should not we abandon doing (using the means) and just rely on the record." He replied, "Go on doing (using the means), for everyone is helped to do that for which he was created.

Those who are among the people of happiness will be helped to do the appropriate deeds of the people of happiness. But those who are among the people of misfortune will be helped to do the appropriate deeds of the people of misfortune." [14]

---

[14] Narrated by Al-Bukhaari and Muslim

The reliance on Allah (awj) is associated with Al-'Ibaadah

Thus, all that Allah (swt) has ordered His 'Ibaad as to the causes is an aspect of 'Ibaadah. And the reliance is associated with A l-'Ibaadah as in the saying of Allah (swt),

فَاعْبُدْهُ وَتَوَكَّلْ عَلَيْهِ

So worship Him (O Muhammad saw) and put your trust in Him.
[Hood:123];

and His (swt) saying,

قُلْ هُوَ رَبِّي لَا إِلَهَ إِلَّا هُوَ عَلَيْهِ تَوَكَّلْتُ وَإِلَيْهِ مَتَابِ

Say: 'He (Allah) is my Lord! None has the right to be worshipped but He! On Him is my trust, and to Him will be my return and repentance.'
[Ar Ra'd:30];

and the saying of Shou'aib,

عَلَيْهِ تَوَكَّلْتُ وَإِلَيْهِ أُنِيبُ

In Him (Allah) I trust and unto Him I repent.
[Hood:88]

Amongst these people, too, is a group who leave the favoured of the deeds but not the duties. Thus they are disparaged accordingly.

The presumption due to the extra-ordinary occurrences

Also, amongst them is a group who become presumptuous by what happens to them of extra ordinary occurrences such as a disclosure, an answer of a supplication which is out of the ordinary, etc. Hence, the person becomes overwhelmed with these matters rather than remaining with what he was commanded to perform as worshipping, thanking, and the like. These matters and the like occur frequently to the people of As-Sulook (spiritual self-discipline) and At-Tawajuh (focused devotion); however, Al 'Abd can save himself from these by perpetually holding fast to Allah's Command with which His Messenger was sent. Az-Zuhree said, "Those who passed of our predecessors used to say: 'The adherence to the Sunnah is a rescue.'" For the Sunnah, as Maalik (RA) has said, is like the ark of Noah, whoever rides it will be rescued and whoever misses it will be drowned.

Holding fast to As-Sunnah is a salvation

Al-'Ibaadah, obedience, uprightness, holding fast to the straight path, and the like of the terms have one sole purpose and have two main principles:

The first of which is: that one should not worship but Allah, and the second is: that he should not worship Him except with what He (swt) commanded and legislated, and should not worship Him (awj) with other than that such as with desires, illusions, and innovations. Allah (swt) said.

فَمَن كَانَ يَرْجُو لِقَاءَ رَبِّهِ فَلْيَعْمَلْ عَمَلًا صَالِحًا وَلَا يُشْرِكْ بِعِبَادَةِ رَبِّهِ أَحَدًا

So whoever hopes for the meeting with his Lord, let him do righteous work and associate none as partner in Al-'Ibaadah of his Lord.
[Al Kahaf: 110];

and He (swt) said,

بَلَىٰ مَنْ أَسْلَمَ وَجْهَهُ لِلَّهِ وَهُوَ مُحْسِنٌ فَلَهُ أَجْرُهُ عِندَ رَبِّهِ وَلَا خَوْفٌ عَلَيْهِمْ وَلَا هُمْ يَحْزَنُونَ

Yes, but whoever submits himself to Allah and he is a good-doer, his reward is with his Lord, on such shall be no fear, nor shall they grieve.

[Al Baqarah:112];

and He (swt) said,

قُلْ إِنَّمَا أَنَا بَشَرٌ مِّثْلُكُمْ يُوحَىٰ إِلَيَّ أَنَّمَا إِلَٰهُكُمْ إِلَٰهٌ وَاحِدٌ ۖ فَمَن كَانَ يَرْجُو لِقَاءَ رَبِّهِ فَلْيَعْمَلْ عَمَلًا صَالِحًا وَلَا يُشْرِكْ بِعِبَادَةِ رَبِّهِ أَحَدًا

And who can be better in Deen than one who submits to Allah, and he is a doer of good (deeds) and follows the way of Ibraaheem, the worshiper of none but Allah Alone? Indeed, Allah did take Ibraaheem as an intimate friend.

[An-Nisaa:125]

Allah (awj) disgraces Al-Bida'

The righteous deed is the beneficence, that is to perform the good deeds. And the good deeds are those which are beloved by Allah (awj) and His Messenger (saw), and which were commanded whether with firm command or favouring command.

Therefore, whatever exists in Ad-Deen by way of innovations which are not in the Scripture, nor in the authentic Sunnah, no matter who said them or practised them, are not legislated. Because Allah (awj) does not love them nor does His Messenger; they ought not to be of the good deeds and the righteous deeds. The same holds for he who does unallowable matters such as blatant sins and injustice. These matters are not of the good deeds and the righteous deeds. As for His (swt) saying,

وَلَا يُشْرِكْ بِعِبَادَةِ رَبِّهِ أَحَدًا

And (let him) associate none as partner in Al 'Ibaadah of his Lord.
[Al-Kahaf:110];

and His (swt) saying,

بَلَىٰ مَنْ أَسْلَمَ وَجْهَهُ لِلَّهِ

He who submits himself to Allah   [Al- Baqarah:112];

that is the sincere devotion of Ad-Deen to Allah Alone. 'Umar bin Al-Khattaab (RAA) used to say, "O Allah! May You make the whole of my deed righteous, and may You make it pure (sincerely devoted) for Your Face, and do not make for anyone else any share from it."

The most devoted and proper deed

Al-Fudhayl bin 'Ayyadh said concerning the saying of Allah (swt)

That He (Allah) may try you as to which of you is best in deed. [Al-Mulk:2],

"The best deed is that which is most devoted and most proper." The people asked, "O Aba 'Alee! How should it be most devoted and most proper?" He said, "For if the deed was devoted but was not proper it would not be accepted, and if it was proper but not devoted it would not be accepted; the devoted is to be for Allah Alone, and the proper is to be in compliance with As-Sunnah."

Adding other commands to Al-'Ibaadah

If it was said: Since all that Allah loves is included in Al-'Ibaadah, why did He (swt) add to it (Al 'Ibaadah) other commands such as in His (swt) saying in the opening of the Scripture,

إِيَّاكَ نَعْبُدُ وَإِيَّاكَ نَسْتَعِينُ

You (Alone) we worship and You (Alone) we ask for help.   [Al-Faatihah:5];

and in His (swt) saying to His Prophet (saw),

فَاعْبُدْهُ وَتَوَكَّلْ عَلَيْهِ

So worship Him (O Muhammad saw) and put your trust in Him.   [Hood: 123];

and the saying of Nooh (to his people),

أَنِ اعْبُدُوا اللَّهَ وَاتَّقُوهُ وَأَطِيعُونِ

You should worship Allah, protect yourselves from Him by warding off evil, and obey me.   [Nooh:3];

and similar to this of the sayings of other Messengers?

Al-Ihsann Wa Al-Munkar - Beneficient deed and reprehensible deed

It is said: This (literary style) is very frequent, as in His (awj) saying,

$$إِنَّ الصَّلَاةَ تَنْهَىٰ عَنِ الْفَحْشَاءِ وَالْمُنكَرِ$$

Verily, As-Salaat prevents from committing Al Fahshaa (blatant sin) and Al-Munkar (reprehensible deeds).   [Al-'Ankaboot:45]

Here Al-Fahshaa (blatant sin) is a part of Al-Munkar (the reprehensible deeds). This occurred also in His (awj) saying,

$$إِنَّ اللَّهَ يَأْمُرُ بِالْعَدْلِ وَالْإِحْسَانِ وَإِيتَاءِ ذِي الْقُرْبَىٰ وَيَنْهَىٰ عَنِ الْفَحْشَاءِ وَالْمُنكَرِ وَالْبَغْيِ$$

Verily! Allah enjoins justice and beneficience, and giving (help) to kith and kin and He forbids Al Fahshaa (blatant sin) and Al-Munkar (reprehensible deeds), and (all kinds of) oppression.   [An-Nahl:90]

Here "giving help to kith and kin" is a part of justice and beneficence, while "blatant sin" and "oppression" are of the reprehensible deeds.

Also, in His (awj) saying,

And as to those who hold fast by the Scripture and establish As-Salaat perfectly. [Al-A'raaf: 170] Whereas establishing As-Salaat is of the greatest forms of holding fast to the Scripture.

Also, in what He (awj) said about His Prophets,

إِنَّهُمْ كَانُوا يُسَارِعُونَ فِي الْخَيْرَاتِ وَيَدْعُونَنَا رَغَبًا وَرَهَبًا

Verily, they used to rush to do good deeds, and they used to call on Us with hope and fear and they used to humble themselves before Us. [Al-Anbiyaa:90]

Their "call with hope and fear" is of doing the good deeds. Examples similar to these are numerous in the Quran.

The meaning of a term varies depending on it being separate or being in conjunction

Concerning this type (of literary style): In certain instances, the latter comes as a part of the former, hence the latter is conjuncted to the former to specify it. In this instance the term is sought in its general meaning as well as in its specific meaning.

In another instance, the use of the term is more diversified. When the term is separate it is generalized, and when it is in conjunction with another, it is specified. For example, the term "Al- Faqeer" (the poor) and the term "Al-Miskeen" (the needy) when one of them is used separately the other is included in it, as in His (swt) saying,

لِلْفُقَرَاءِ الَّذِينَ أُحْصِرُوا فِي سَبِيلِ اللَّهِ

(Charity is) for the poor, who in Allah's Cause are restricted (from travel).

[Al-Baqarah:273]

and his (awj) saying,

فَكَفَّارَتُهُ إِطْعَامُ عَشَرَةِ مَسَاكِينَ

Or feeding ten needy persons.　　　　　　　[Al-Maaidah:89]

But when they were used in conjuction with each other as in His (swt) saying, *Alms are only for the poor, the needy, and...* [At-

Tawbah:60]

they became of two different types.

It has been also said: when the specific is conjuncted to the general the specific does not enter in the general in that instance; it is rather of the same type.

But the investigation of this matter shows that this statement is not necessarily true. Allah (swt) said,

مَن كَانَ عَدُوًّا لِّلَّهِ وَمَلَائِكَتِهِ وَرُسُلِهِ وَجِبْرِيلَ وَمِيكَالَ فَإِنَّ اللَّهَ عَدُوٌّ لِّلْكَافِرِينَ

Whoever is an enemy to Allah and His angels and His messengers and Gabriel and Michael - then indeed, Allah is an enemy to the disbelievers.

[Al Baqarah:98];

and He (swt) said,

وَإِذْ أَخَذْنَا مِنَ النَّبِيِّينَ مِيثَاقَهُمْ وَمِنكَ وَمِن نُّوحٍ وَإِبْرَاهِيمَ وَمُوسَىٰ وَعِيسَى ابْنِ مَرْيَمَ

And (remember) when We took from the prophets their covenant and from you (O Muhammad saw) and from Nooh, Ibraaheem, Musa, and 'Eesa bin Maryam.
[Al-Ahzaab:7]

Mentioning the specific with the general can be for a variety of reasons. First, it might be because of a certain speciality which does not exist in the rest of the individuals which form the general, as was in the case of Nooh, Ibraheem, Musa and 'Eesa. In another time, it might be because the general is indefinite and one cannot understand the detail of its generality as in His (swt) saying,

الَّذِينَ يُؤْمِنُونَ بِالْغَيْبِ وَيُقِيمُونَ الصَّلَاةَ وَمِمَّا رَزَقْنَاهُمْ يُنفِقُونَ – وَالَّذِينَ يُؤْمِنُونَ بِمَا أُنزِلَ إِلَيْكَ وَمَا أُنزِلَ مِن قَبْلِكَ وَبِالْآخِرَةِ هُمْ يُوقِنُونَ

A guidance to those who are protecting themselves from the punishment of Allah by warding off evil. Who believe in al-Ghayb (the Unseen), establish As-Salaat, and spend out of what We have provided for them. And who believe in that which has been sent down (revealed) to you (Muhammad SAWS) and in that which was sent down (revealed) before you.   [Al-Baqarah:3-4]

His saying "They believe in *al-Ghayb* (the Unseen)" comprises all the unseen which one should believe in; however it is rather indefinite. There is not in it any indication that part of the Unseen is: "What has been revealed to you (Muhammad SAWS) and what has been revealed before you." It might also mean that they believe in the reported subject, that is *al-Ghayb*, and in the reporting about *al-Ghayb*, and that is "what has been revealed to you (Muhammad SAWS) and what has been revealed before you."

Making explicit and unclear generality

Mentioning the specific with the general can be for a variety of reasons. First, it might be because of a certain speciality which does not exist in the rest of the individuals which form the general, as was in the case of Nooh, Ibraheem, Musa and 'Eesa. In another time, it might be because the general is indefinite and one cannot understand the detail of its generality as in His (swt) saying,

الَّذِينَ يُؤْمِنُونَ بِالْغَيْبِ وَيُقِيمُونَ الصَّلَاةَ وَمِمَّا رَزَقْنَاهُمْ يُنفِقُونَ – وَالَّذِينَ يُؤْمِنُونَ بِمَا أُنزِلَ إِلَيْكَ وَمَا أُنزِلَ مِن قَبْلِكَ وَبِالْآخِرَةِ هُمْ يُوقِنُونَ

A guidance to those who are protecting themselves from the punishment of Allah by warding off evil. Who believe in al-Ghayb (the Unseen), establish As-Salaat, and spend out of what We have provided for them. And who believe in that which has been sent down (revealed) to you (Muhammad SAWS) and in that which was sent down (revealed) before you. [Al-Baqarah:3-4]

His saying "They believe in *al-Ghayb* (the Unseen)" comprises all the unseen which one should believe in; however, it is rather indefinite. There is not in it any indication that part of the Unseen is: "What has been revealed to you (Muhammad SAWS) and what has been revealed before you." It might also mean that they believe in the reported subject, that is *al-Ghayb*, and in the reporting about *al-Ghayb*, and that is "what has been revealed to you (Muhammad SAWS) and what has been revealed before you."

Distinguishing As-Salaat because of its distinguishable qualification in the 'Ibaadah

Also under this topic is the saying of Allah (swt),

$$اتْلُ مَا أُوحِيَ إِلَيْكَ مِنَ الْكِتَابِ وَأَقِمِ الصَّلَاةَ$$

Recite what is sent to you of the Scripture by revelation (i.e. the Qur'an), and establish As-Salaat.   [Al- 'Ankaboot:45];

and His (awj) saying,

$$وَالَّذِينَ يُمَسِّكُونَ بِالْكِتَابِ وَأَقَامُوا الصَّلَاةَ$$

And those who hold fast by the Scripture and establish As-Salaat.
[Al-A'raaf:170]

The recitation of the Scripture is: following it and implementing it, as Ibn Mas'ood has said concerning the saying of Allah (swt),

Those to whom We have given the Scripture recite It as It should be recited, [Al-Baqarah:121], he said, "They allow its allowable, they forbid its prohibitions, they believe in its unclear allegorical passages, and they implement its firm (verses)."

Therefore, following the Scripture comprises As-Salat and others. However, He (swt) specifically mentioned it because of its distinguishable qualification.

Parts of Al-'Ibaadah are specifically mentioned to be sought for its own qualifications

Also His (awj) saying to Musa

إِنَّنِي أَنَا اللَّهُ لَا إِلَهَ إِلَّا أَنَا فَاعْبُدْنِي وَأَقِمِ الصَّلَاةَ لِذِكْرِي

Verily! I am Allah, there is no deity but I, so worship Me and establish As-Salaat for My remembrance, [Ta Ha:14],

here establishing As Salaat for His (swt) remembrance is of the most exalted 'Ibaadah of Him (awj). Also, in His (swt) saying,

يَا أَيُّهَا الَّذِينَ آمَنُوا اتَّقُوا اللَّهَ وَقُولُوا قَوْلًا سَدِيدًا

Protect yourself from the punishment of Allah by warding off evil and say always a righteous saying.   [Al-Ahzaab:71],

and His (swt) saying,

يَا أَيُّهَا الَّذِينَ آمَنُوا اتَّقُوا اللَّهَ وَابْتَغُوا إِلَيْهِ الْوَسِيلَةَ

Protect yourself from Allah by warding off evil and seek the means of approach to Him.   [Al-Maa idah:35],

and His (swt) saying,

يَا أَيُّهَا الَّذِينَ آمَنُوا اتَّقُوا اللَّهَ وَكُونُوا مَعَ الصَّادِقِينَ

Protect yourself from Allah by warding off evil and be with the truthful.

[At-Tawbah: 119],

for all these matters are part of the complement of At-Taqwa.

Also, His (swt) saying,

$$\text{فَاعْبُدْهُ وَتَوَكَّلْ عَلَيْهِ}$$

So worship Him (Allah) and put your trust in Him.   [Hood:123]

For the reliance is indeed seeking help, which is of worshipping Him (awj). However, it was specifically mentioned to be sought by the one who is performing Al-'Ibaadah because of its specific qualification: it is the aid by which one performs other aspects of 'Ibaadah, for He the Exalted cannot be worshipped without His help.

The perfection of the created one is his realization of *Al-'Uboodiyah* for Allah (swt)

If this statement becomes clear, the perfection of the creature is dependent on the realization of his *'Uboodiyah* to Allah (awj). The more Al-'Abd realizes *Al-'Uboodiyah* the more his perfection will increase and the more his rank will be high. Whoever imagined that the creature can depart from *Al 'Uboodiyah* in any of its aspects, or that departing from it is more perfect, he will be of the most ignorant amongst all the creation. Such a one will be the most astray amongst them. Allah (swt) said,

وَقَالُوا اتَّخَذَ الرَّحْمَٰنُ وَلَدًا ۗ سُبْحَانَهُ ۚ بَلْ عِبَادٌ مُّكْرَمُونَ – لَا يَسْبِقُونَهُ بِالْقَوْلِ وَهُم بِأَمْرِهِ يَعْمَلُونَ – يَعْلَمُ مَا بَيْنَ أَيْدِيهِمْ وَمَا خَلْفَهُمْ وَلَا يَشْفَعُونَ إِلَّا لِمَنِ ارْتَضَىٰ وَهُم مِّنْ خَشْيَتِهِ مُشْفِقُونَ

And they say: 'The Beneficent (Allah) has begotten children.' Exalted be He! Those whom they call children, (i.e. angels), are but honored 'Ibaad. They speak not until He has spoken, and they act by His command. He knows what is before them, and what is behind them, and they cannot intercede except for him with whom He is pleased. And they stand in awe due to their apprehension of Him.

[Al Anbiyaa:26-28];

and He (swt) said.

لَّقَدْ جِئْتُمْ شَيْئًا إِدًّا – تَكَادُ السَّمَاوَاتُ يَتَفَطَّرْنَ مِنْهُ وَتَنشَقُّ الْأَرْضُ وَتَخِرُّ الْجِبَالُ هَدًّا – أَن دَعَوْا لِلرَّحْمَٰنِ وَلَدًا – وَمَا يَنبَغِي لِلرَّحْمَٰنِ أَن يَتَّخِذَ وَلَدًا – إِن كُلُّ مَن فِي السَّمَاوَاتِ وَالْأَرْضِ إِلَّا آتِي الرَّحْمَٰنِ عَبْدًا – لَّقَدْ أَحْصَاهُمْ وَعَدَّهُمْ عَدًّا – وَكُلُّهُمْ آتِيهِ يَوْمَ الْقِيَامَةِ فَرْدًا

Indeed you have brought forth a terrible thing. Whereby almost the heavens are torn and the earth is split asunder and the mountains fall in ruins. That you ascribed children to the Beneficient (Allah). But it is not suitable for (the Majesty of) the Beneficient (Allah) that He should beget children. There is none in the heavens and the earth but comes unto the Beneficient (Allah) as a subdued 'Abd. Verily He knows their number and has counted them a full counting. And every one of them will come to Him alone, on the Day of Resurrection. [Mariyam:89-95]

'Eesa (Jesus saw) was no more than a 'Abd

And He (swt) said concerning the Maseeh (the Messiah),

إِنْ هُوَ إِلَّا عَبْدٌ أَنْعَمْنَا عَلَيْهِ وَجَعَلْنَاهُ مَثَلًا لِّبَنِي إِسْرَائِيلَ

Verily he ('Eesa saw) was no more than a worshiper. We granted Our favor to him, and We made him an example to the children of Israa-eel.

[Az-Zukhruf:59];

"Surely those who are near to your Lord are never too proud
to worship Him (swt)"

وَلَهُ مَن فِي السَّمَاوَاتِ وَالْأَرْضِ ۖ وَمَنْ عِندَهُ لَا يَسْتَكْبِرُونَ عَنْ عِبَادَتِهِ وَلَا
يَسْتَحْسِرُونَ – يُسَبِّحُونَ اللَّيْلَ وَالنَّهَارَ لَا يَفْتُرُونَ 0

*And to Him (Allah) belongs whosoever is in the heavens and the
earth. And those who are in His very presence are not too proud to
worship Him, nor are they weary (of His 'Ibaadah). They exalt Him
night and day (and) they never slacken (to do so).*   [Al-Anbiyaa:
19-20];

and He (SVVT) said,

لَّن يَسْتَنكِفَ الْمَسِيحُ أَن يَكُونَ عَبْدًا لِّلَّهِ وَلَا الْمَلَائِكَةُ الْمُقَرَّبُونَ ۚ وَمَن
يَسْتَنكِفْ عَنْ عِبَادَتِهِ وَيَسْتَكْبِرْ فَسَيَحْشُرُهُمْ إِلَيْهِ جَمِيعًا – فَأَمَّا الَّذِينَ آمَنُوا
وَعَمِلُوا الصَّالِحَاتِ فَيُوَفِّيهِمْ أُجُورَهُمْ وَيَزِيدُهُم مِّن فَضْلِهِ ۖ وَأَمَّا الَّذِينَ
اسْتَنكَفُوا وَاسْتَكْبَرُوا فَيُعَذِّبُهُمْ عَذَابًا أَلِيمًا وَلَا يَجِدُونَ لَهُم مِّن دُونِ اللَّهِ وَلِيًّا
وَلَا نَصِيرًا

*Al-Maseeh will never be proud as not to be a 'Abd to Allah, nor even
the Angels who are near (to Allah). And whosoever refuses His
'Ibaadah and is proud, He (Allah) will gather them all together unto
Himself. So as for those who believed and did righteous deeds, He
will give them their (due) rewards, and more, out of His Bounty.*

But as for those who refuse His 'Ibaadah and were proud, He will punish them with a painful torment and they will not find for themselves besides Allah any protector or helper. [An-Nisaa: 172-173];

Those who scorn My 'Ibaadah will surely enter Hell in humiliation

وَقَالَ رَبُّكُمُ ادْعُونِي أَسْتَجِبْ لَكُمْ ۚ إِنَّ الَّذِينَ يَسْتَكْبِرُونَ عَنْ عِبَادَتِي سَيَدْخُلُونَ جَهَنَّمَ دَاخِرِينَ

And your Lord said: 'Invoke Me, and I will respond to your (invocation). Verily! Those who scorn My 'Ibaadah will surely enter Hell in humiliation.'

[Al Moo-min:60];

and He (swt) said,

وَمِنْ آيَاتِهِ اللَّيْلُ وَالنَّهَارُ وَالشَّمْسُ وَالْقَمَرُ ۚ لَا تَسْجُدُوا لِلشَّمْسِ وَلَا لِلْقَمَرِ وَاسْجُدُوا لِلَّهِ الَّذِي خَلَقَهُنَّ إِن كُنتُمْ إِيَّاهُ تَعْبُدُونَ – فَإِنِ اسْتَكْبَرُوا فَالَّذِينَ عِندَ رَبِّكَ يُسَبِّحُونَ لَهُ بِاللَّيْلِ وَالنَّهَارِ وَهُمْ لَا يَسْأَمُونَ

And from among His Signs are the night and the day, and the sun and the moon. Prostrate not to the sun nor to the moon, but prostrate to Allah Who created them if you (really) worship Him. But if they are too proud (to do so), then there are those who are with your Lord (Angels) exalting Him night and day and never are they tired.

[Fussilat:37-38];

and He (swt) said,

وَاذْكُر رَّبَّكَ فِي نَفْسِكَ تَضَرُّعًا وَخِيفَةً وَدُونَ الْجَهْرِ مِنَ الْقَوْلِ بِالْغُدُوِّ وَالْآصَالِ وَلَا تَكُن مِّنَ الْغَافِلِينَ – إِنَّ الَّذِينَ عِندَ رَبِّكَ لَا يَسْتَكْبِرُونَ عَنْ عِبَادَتِهِ وَيُسَبِّحُونَهُ وَلَهُ يَسْجُدُونَ

And (O Muhammad saw) remember your Lord in your (very) soul, humbly and with fear, without loudness in words in the momings and evenings, and be not of those who are neglectful. Surely those who are near to your Lord are never too proud to worship Him, and they exalt Him and prostrate before Him.

[Al-A'raaf:205-206];

Describing thc best of the creation with Al-'Ibaadah

These verses and their like, in which the best of the creation are described with Al-'Ibaadah and those who deviate from that are condemned, are numerous in the Quran. Indeed, Allah (swt) informed that He sent all the Messengers with that. He (swt) said,

وَمَا أَرْسَلْنَا مِن قَبْلِكَ مِن رَّسُولٍ إِلَّا نُوحِي إِلَيْهِ أَنَّهُ لَا إِلَٰهَ إِلَّا أَنَا فَاعْبُدُونِ

And We did not send any Messenger before you (O Muhammad saw) but We revealed to Him (saying): 'There is none worthy of being worshipped but I (Allah), so worship Me (Alone and none else).'   [Al-Anbiyaa:25];

and He (swt) said,

وَلَقَدْ بَعَثْنَا فِي كُلِّ أُمَّةٍ رَّسُولًا أَنِ اعْبُدُوا اللَّهَ وَاجْتَنِبُوا الطَّاغُوتَ

And verily We have sent amongst every nation a Messenger (saying): 'Worship Allah (Alone), and avoid all false deities. [An-Nahl:36];

and He (swt) said to Beni Israa-eel,

يَا عِبَادِيَ الَّذِينَ آمَنُوا إِنَّ أَرْضِي وَاسِعَةٌ فَإِيَّايَ فَاعْبُدُونِ

O My 'Ibaad who believe! Certainly, spacious is My earth. Therefore worship Me (Alone).   [Al 'Ankaboot:56];

and,

And protect yourselves from Me by warding off evil. [Al-Baqarah]; and He (swt) said,

يَا أَيُّهَا النَّاسُ اعْبُدُوا رَبَّكُمُ الَّذِي خَلَقَكُمْ وَالَّذِينَ مِن قَبْلِكُمْ لَعَلَّكُمْ تَتَّقُونَ

O mankind! Worship your Lord, Who created you and those who were before you so that you may protect yourself from Me. [Al-Baqarah:21];

and He (swt) said.

وَمَا خَلَقْتُ الْجِنَّ وَالْإِنسَ إِلَّا لِيَعْبُدُونِ

And I created not the Jinns and men except that they should worship Me (Alone). [Adth- Dthaariyaat:56];

The call of the Messenger to worship Allah (awj)

قُلْ إِنِّي أُمِرْتُ أَنْ أَعْبُدَ اللَّهَ مُخْلِصًا لَّهُ الدِّينَ – وَأُمِرْتُ لِأَنْ أَكُونَ أَوَّلَ الْمُسْلِمِينَ – قُلْ إِنِّي أَخَافُ إِنْ عَصَيْتُ رَبِّي عَذَابَ يَوْمٍ عَظِيمٍ – قُلِ اللَّهَ أَعْبُدُ مُخْلِصًا لَّهُ دِينِي – فَاعْبُدُوا مَا شِئْتُم مِّن دُونِهِ ۗ

Say (O Muhammad saw): 'Verily, I am commanded to worship Allah (Alone) by making Ad Deen pure for Him only. And I am commanded to be the first of those who are Muslims (those who surrender to Allah).' Say: 'Verily, I fear, if I disobey my Lord, the torment of a great Day.' Say: 'Allah alone I worship making my Deen pure for Him. Then worship what you like besides Him.'

[Az-Zumar: 11-15]

Everyone of the Messengers opened his *Da'wah* with the call to worship Allah (awj)

Everyone of the Messengers opened his *Da'wah* with the invitation to worship Allah, as is the saying of Nooh (saw) and those who came after him in Surat Ash-Shu'araa and others,

$$أَنِ اعْبُدُوا اللَّهَ مَا لَكُم مِّنْ إِلَهٍ غَيْرُهُ$$

Worship Allah! you have no other deity but Him.   [Al-Moo-minoon:32]

In the "Musnad" upon Ibn 'Umar (RAA), upon the Prophet (saw) who said, "I was sent between the hands of the Hour with the sword until Allah will be worshipped Alone with no partner, my sustenance was made under the shadow of my spear, and humiliation and lowliness were made for those who disobey my order." [15]

---

[15] Narrated as Mu'allaq by Al-Bukhaari and Abu Dawud Al Haafidthh Ibn Hajar said: its Isnaad is Hasan

Defining the chosen guided 'Ibaad of Allah (awj)

He (swt) has shown that His chosen 'Ibaad are those who will escape the mischiefs which are adorned by Ash-Shaitaan (Satan). Ash-Shaitaan said,

O my Lord! Because You misled meI shall indeed adorn the path of error for them (mankind) on earth and I shall mislead them all. Except for Your chosen, guided 'Ibaad among them. [Al-Hijr: 39-40]

قَالَ هَٰذَا صِرَاطٌ عَلَيَّ مُسْتَقِيمٌ – إِنَّ عِبَادِي لَيْسَ لَكَ عَلَيْهِمْ سُلْطَانٌ إِلَّا مَنِ اتَّبَعَكَ مِنَ الْغَاوِينَ

Allah (swt) said, This is a Way which will be straight and well guarded by Me. Certainly you shall have no authority over my 'Ibaad, except those who follow you of the wrong-doers. [Al-Hijr: 41-42]

قَالَ فَبِعِزَّتِكَ لَأُغْوِيَنَّهُمْ أَجْمَعِينَ – إِلَّا عِبَادَكَ مِنْهُمُ الْمُخْلَصِينَ

Also he (Ash-Shaitaan) said, Thus I swear by Your Might (O Allah) that I shall mislead them all except your chosen 'Ibaad amongst them. [Saad: 82-83]

And Allah (swt) said regarding Yoosuf (saw),

كَذَٰلِكَ لِنَصْرِفَ عَنْهُ السُّوءَ وَالْفَحْشَاءَ ۚ إِنَّهُ مِنْ عِبَادِنَا الْمُخْلَصِينَ

Thus (did We order) that We might turn away from him evil and the blatant sin (i.e. adultery). Surely he was one of Our chosen 'Ibaad

[Yoosuf: 24]

سُبْحَانَ اللَّهِ عَمَّا يَصِفُونَ – إِلَّا عِبَادَ اللَّهِ الْمُخْلَصِينَ

And He (swt) said, Exalted be Allah from what they ascribe (to Him). (And the Jinn knew that the Qureish pagans will be punished) except the chosen 'Ibaad of Allah. [As-Saafaat: 159-160]

إِنَّهُ لَيْسَ لَهُ سُلْطَانٌ عَلَى الَّذِينَ آمَنُوا وَعَلَىٰ رَبِّهِمْ يَتَوَكَّلُونَ – إِنَّمَا سُلْطَانُهُ عَلَى الَّذِينَ يَتَوَلَّوْنَهُ وَالَّذِينَ هُم بِهِ مُشْرِكُونَ

Also, He (swt) said, Verily! He (Ash-Shaitaan) has no power over those who believe and put their trust only in their Lord (Allah). His power is only over those who take him as an ally and those who because of him join partners (with Allah).   [An-Nahl: 99-100]

Describing those whom He (swt) has selected amongst His creation with *Al-'Uboodiyah*

And with *Al-'Uboodiyah* He (awj) described those whom He (swt) has selected amongst His creation as stated in His saying.

وَاذْكُرْ عِبَادَنَا إِبْرَاهِيمَ وَإِسْحَاقَ وَيَعْقُوبَ أُولِي الْأَيْدِي وَالْأَبْصَارِ – إِنَّا أَخْلَصْنَاهُم بِخَالِصَةٍ ذِكْرَى الدَّارِ – وَإِنَّهُمْ عِندَنَا لَمِنَ الْمُصْطَفَيْنَ الْأَخْيَارِ

And remember Our 'Ibaad, Ibraaheem, Ishaaq and Ya'qoob, possessors of beneficence (to their people) and understanding (of Ad-Deen). Verily, We did choose them by granting them a special thing: the remembrance of Ad-Daar (the home of the Hereafter). And they are in Our sight, verily of the chosen and the best. [Saad:45-47];

and in His (swt) saying,

وَاذْكُرْ عَبْدَنَا دَاوُودَ ذَا الْأَيْدِ ۖ إِنَّهُ أَوَّابٌ

And remember Our 'Abd Daawood, the possessor of beneficience. Verily! He was ever oft-turning in repentance (toward Allah). [Saad:17];

'Abd is an attribute of honor for all the Prophets

And He (swt) said concerning Sulaimaan,

وَوَهَبْنَا لِدَاوُودَ سُلَيْمَانَ ۚ نِعْمَ الْعَبْدُ ۖ إِنَّهُ أَوَّابٌ

How excellent an 'Abd. Verily he was ever oft turning in repentance (to Us)!

[Saad:30];

and concerning Ayoob He (swt) said,

نِّعْمَ الْعَبْدُ ۖ

How excellent an 'Abd.   [Saad:44];

and also He (swt) said about him,

وَاذْكُرْ عَبْدَنَا أَيُّوبَ إِذْ نَادَىٰ رَبَّهُ

And remember Our 'Abd Ayoob when he invoked his Lord.
[Saad:41]

Regarding Nooh (AS) He (swt) said,

ذُرِّيَّةَ مَنْ حَمَلْنَا مَعَ نُوحٍ ۚ إِنَّهُ كَانَ عَبْدًا شَكُورًا

O offspring of those whom We carried (in the ark) with Nooh!
Verily he was a grateful 'Abd. [Al Israa:3];

Ascribing *Al-'Uboodiyah* to the Seal of the Prophets

And He (awj) said concerning the Seal of His Messengers,

سُبْحَانَ الَّذِي أَسْرَىٰ بِعَبْدِهِ لَيْلًا مِّنَ الْمَسْجِدِ الْحَرَامِ إِلَى الْمَسْجِدِ الْأَقْصَى

Exalted be He (Allah) who took His 'Abd (Muhammad saw) for a Journey by night from the Sacred Mosque (of Mekkah) to the Farthest Mosque (in Beit Al-Maqdes).   [Al-Israa: 1];

and He (swt) said,

وَأَنَّهُ لَمَّا قَامَ عَبْدُ اللَّهِ

And when 'Aba-u-Allah (Muhammad saw) stood up calling unto Him (Allah Alone).   [Al Jinn: 19];

and He (swt) said.

وَإِن كُنتُمْ فِي رَيْبٍ مِّمَّا نَزَّلْنَا عَلَىٰ عَبْدِنَا

And if you are in doubt of what we have revealed unto Our 'Abd.   [Al-Baqarah:23];

and He (swt) said.

$$\text{فَأَوْحَىٰ إِلَىٰ عَبْدِهِ مَا أَوْحَىٰ}$$

So did he (Jibreel) reveal to His (Allah's) 'Abd what has been revealed (then).

[An-Najm:10];

and He (swt) said,

$$\text{عَيْنًا يَشْرَبُ بِهَا عِبَادُ اللَّهِ}$$

A spring, where from 'Ibaad-u-Allah shall drink.   [Ad-Dahr:6];

and He (swt) said,

$$\text{وَعِبَادُ الرَّحْمَٰنِ الَّذِينَ يَمْشُونَ عَلَى الْأَرْضِ هَوْنًا}$$

And the 'Ibaad of the Most Beneficient (Allah) are those who walk on earth in humility.   [Al Furqaan:63]

The verses which are similar to these are many and numerous in the Quran.

The end of Part I of *Al-'Uboodiyah* - The Essay of Worship by Ibn Taymiyah

Dar Ul Thaqafah
www.darulthaqafah.com
https://twitter.com/darulthaqafah
Email: darulthaqafah@gmail.com

Find our titles on your favourite online bookstore using the keyword 'Dar Ul Thaqafah'

Translation of the Qur'ān

It should be perfectly clear that the Qur'ān is only authentic in its original language, Arabic. Since perfect translation of the Qur'ān is impossible, we have used the translation of the meaning of the Qur'ān throughout the book, as the result is only a crude meaning of the Arabic text.

Qur'ānic verses appear in speech marks proceeded by a reference to the Surah and verse number. Sayings (Hadith) of Prophet Muhammad (saw) appear in inverted commas along with reference to the Hadith Book and its Reporter.

Al Uboodiyah

Being a True Slave of Allah

Taqiudin Ibn Taymiyah

Translated By
Abdallah M. Mekkaoui

Printed by BoD™in Norderstedt, Germany